Responses from R

"Your essays are prof
MW01100712

"Thank you for publishing your WebPage. It has helped me intellectually identify what I intuitively know Mormonism is."

"I have read the information on your site and found you did an excellent job in describing the impossible."

"Your website is wonderful! What a joy it is to see intellectual freedom from someone so obviously intelligent. It seems that your intellect was confined for so long that it finally had to explode."

"I have truly enjoyed reading your articles on the website. I have had many of the same feelings about the Mormon Church and its attitude toward women."

"You have done an excellent job of writing down your way out of the maze. I read all of your writing with great interest. No doubt I will have to re-read most of it again ... and again."

"Thank you so much for your site "LIFE AFTER MORMONISM and THE DOUBLE-BIND." I found the site to be one of the better, more true to life pages to read in my decision to leave the church."

"I just wanted to commend you on your site. ... I was moved by what I found. You can be assured that the truth speaks loud and clear in your words."

"I am really blown away. This is an interesting web site."

"What you have done here is amazing."

The Pattern
of
The Double-Bind

An Enigma

Back to back they faced each other,
Drew their swords and shot each other.

in

Mormonism

Marion Stricker

The Pattern of The Double-Bind in Mormonism

Universal Publishers/uPUBLISH.com

USA • 2000

ISBN: 1-58112-739-1

www.upublish.com/books/stricker.htm

To Matt. Thank you
for *being there.*

Table of Contents

Preface

"Problems can't be solved until they are discovered."

~ Edwin G. Boring

How this Book Came to Be

This book is the culmination of a twenty-year odyssey, a personal quest for a solution to an unknown problem that had become emotionally and intellectually intolerable for me. My main symptom was that I could never quite think, or do things "right" – I felt and thought that something must be terribly wrong with my mind, because significant *others* could always set things "right" for me; therefore, I must be "stupid." It was implied that my problem wasn't shared by others; I was told that it was I who needed to change, not they. I believed this assessment. But if I needed to change, how could I – if I didn't know what my problem was? My search began with three questions: What was wrong with me? What was my problem? Does it have a name? I was willing to abide by whatever I found to be true. What I found through trial and error, following threads and connections, was a pattern of behavior I finally identified and named *The Pattern of the Double-Bind*.

What I also discovered was that I was not alone in my dilemma; as I continued, *The Pattern* began to reveal Universal implications. At first, I found that my loved ones, and others in Mormonism, were also trapped inside it, unknowingly; this created an urge to find its origins. It was in this extended search that I found that *The Pattern* went way beyond my own personal experiences in Mormonism.

The Pattern is not obvious, the reason being that its insidious nature operates silently with powerful cultural taboos and customs contained within it: one must not see, hear, speak, or question anything contrary to its unexamined "truth." Once I had discovered *The Pattern* in my own life, it was particularly painful to realize that I had "voluntarily" cooperated, as an "accomplice," in perpetuating a lie – a lie masked as a truth.

The Church of Jesus Christ of Latter-day Saints, better known as the Mormon Church – and also referred to as Mormonism – contains, as its psychological basis, this Pattern. I was raised almost exclusively within its environment, was married in the Mormon Temple (1950), raised six children, and was to live a life dedicated to the death covenants exacted in the Temple. Mormonism is not the only corporation of its kind to be based on this Pattern, but it is where I first discovered it.

In extending the ramifications of *The Pattern* to its logical end it is found that it causes the very problems it claims to be able to cure – by the use of the cause! It is a circular system used to control others which reverses the possible evolution towards intellectual integrity – a form of *de-evolution*, and in its extreme form leads to mental havoc and possible madness. Yet, at the same time, it claims to be the means of obtaining peace of mind through "intelligence." In other words, *The Pattern* is a form of illogical "logic." Needless to say, I found out what was "wrong" with me; my ability to think rationally, to question, was condemning me.

The cure for this madness is its opposite – it is to be able to reason without fear. This is made possible by the exposure and understanding of the cause; hence, the aim of this book – to expose the nature of *The Pattern* and to show how it is possible to live a life relatively free from its web of deceit.

Part I describes *The Nature of The Pattern and the Double-Bind*; it defines and gives examples of what the Double-Bind is, how it is used in different stages – and the results incurred. Part II presents examples of personal experiences of *The Pattern of The Double-Bind in Mormonism*, which includes the double-bind, the hub around which The Pattern revolves. This is followed by Part

III, *My Mormon Crisis*, plus my first personal, *conscious Awakening to The Pattern*. Finally, Part IV gives a *Summary* of The Pattern and its antidote ... in *How to Free Oneself from The Pattern*.

Knowing and understanding the stages involved in *The Pattern of the Double-Bind* help to clear and lift the mind and emotions to an aerial view where it is possible to claim more fully one's personal Identity, which the use of The Pattern destroys – whether that use is perpetrated consciously or unconsciously.

What follows is my attempt to explain this *illogical logic* ... logically.

Part I

The Nature of The Pattern of The Double-Bind

What The Pattern Is and What it Does

The Pattern is a method used that subjugates and dehumanizes. It does this by creating a new fabricated world, the direct opposite of this real world.

A REVIEW OF THE FACTS KNOWN IN THE REAL WORLD

The Basic Necessities for a Constructive Life are:

1. First, our **BODY** ... which houses and cooperates with ...

2. Our **SENSES** ... by which we perceive the real world and which in turn send concrete messages to ...

3. Our **BRAIN** ... which can then function in order to question and reason, which leads to *Self*-control over our own lives ... to make individual choices which are our means of survival as rational, individually aware *human* beings.

This is an **OPEN SYSTEM**, where there is always room for growth, expansion, and correction ... trial and error being included in the process of gaining more awareness and knowledge, which makes possible more life and happiness in its most constructive aspects.

ON THE CONTRARY

The Pattern destroys the awareness of all the above necessary faculties for the realization of our own individual identity; the most essential parts of us as *human* beings are missing. Therefore, all that is human and intrinsic to life, liberty, and the pursuit of happiness, is invalidated. The Pattern destroys *Identity*, along with *integrity of mind*, and the ability to *truly love*.

IT DOES THIS BY TURNING THE REAL WORLD UPSIDE-DOWN

THROUGH FRAUD AND THEFT

It operates by reversing the order of our natural functions, and by "replacement," as follows:

1. The **MIND** of a controller, whom I call the "Binder," reverses the basic order, and replaces the individual's *brain* with the Mind of the Binder; as a result, sense perceptions to the brain are invalidated.

2. **"FEELINGS"** that are attached to the pre-conceived ideas in the Binder's Mind replace individual *authentic perceptions* and their accompanying *emotions.*

3. The **BODY** of the individual is now last in order, and becomes the property of the Binder, and is his to control, replacing *Self*-control.

This is a **CLOSED SYSTEM**, which admits nothing that is not already preconceived by the Binder. To do this, the Binder must continually suppress the integrity of the body, separating the brain and emotions from the real world of *sense perceptions* ... our *means* of perceiving the real world.

THE SCENARIO

The following scenario depicts the different stages in the Pattern.

The Players

The Pattern is a Tragedy in nine scenes, or stages. The main characters are essentially two. The dominant character is an authoritarian male figure called a "Binder"; the other character is called the "Bound" and is dependent on the "Binder."

The Plot

The Pattern is the method of psychological manipulation the Binder uses to bind another to him. This manipulation, going through three previous stages, reaches a crisis in the Double-Bind (Stage 4). From that point on, the Double-Bind is then reinforced by alternate contradictions that obfuscate and deny the Bound his or her ability to *think* or *feel* rationally. The crucial point is reached when the opposites of logical and illogical merge as one. This is followed by the complete fusing of the Bound to the Binder, in a pseudo *"voluntary"* union of mind, which is the complete loss of the individual identity of the Bound.

What The Pattern does, in effect, is to turn the independent, rational mind around so that the Bound reflects only the mind of the Binder, as in a mirror. It creates a whole new orientation to the world, a conversion from the logical to the illogical ... the Real to the unreal ... from Truth to lie.

THE ENACTMENT OF THE PATTERN

A Tragedy in Nine Scenes

Scene 1. The Situation: An individual has a problem

This person has a deep–seated need and seeks a solution to a problem which is affecting her, or his, quest for well-being and happiness. *(I will refer to this character as a woman, but inferring a man, as well; the stages are the same for both.)*

Having had no previous experience to guide her, and going into unknown territory, as it were, she seeks out those who seem to know and have solutions that would fit her needs.

Scene 2. A meeting: The Joint Agreement

The woman is with a found contractor who has designed a way to meet her needs; her main goal has been specified. The contractor states that he has the ability and experience to meet these requirements. His word is accepted and an agreement is made. She contracts to pay for what she, as the purchaser, has ordered. The contractor, in turn, will be working for her and will be paid in full when he has completed his assignment. The woman is relieved, trusts the contractor, and begins to work so that she will be able to pay him for his labor.

Scene 3. A special meeting is called. The contractor has a problem. "Yes, but ..."

"Yes," he knows that he is the contractor *"but,"* in the middle of the project he finds he needs the purchaser's help because an *"emergency"* has come up, and he must leave immediately to complete a previous assignment. The woman agrees to aid the contractor – in this *particular* instance; she is desirous that there should be no unnecessary delays. He leaves, but does not supply her with the necessary *means* to comply. The contractor returns; she has done her best to keep her promise to help him *"but,"* something is wrong; she has *failed* to do properly what was expected of her. She now is expected, again, to honor *her* promise to aid him by doing it *"right"* this time, as the contractor still has *"others who need him more than she does."*

Identity Crisis

This is the stage of transition; the purchaser is unknowingly becoming the "contractor," and the contractor is becoming the "purchaser" *"but ..."* still *claiming* to be the "contractor" while most of the work is now being done by the woman; roles are blurred.   Other names that identify this transitional stage are "Ambiguity" and "Mind-Bind." It is at this turning point that a deviation from Reason and the Real World to the world of fabrication begins, facilitated by the confusion of roles. *This is the wedge that enters the mind which creates Self-doubt and unearned guilt, dividing the mind between "yes" and "no."* The principles of Truth and Honesty are being eroded through Ambiguity.   Trust in an agreement in the Real World is being reversed and replaced with faith in a capricious "contractor."

The woman is eager for the results of the joint agreement and wants to trust, but by having *faith* in, and clinging to, the contractor's *"Yes."* She is willing to put forth additional effort since they are half way through the project and she has put too much energy into it to turn back now; if she did, all that she had worked for, so far, would be wasted; her needs would not be fulfilled; plus, she would have to start all over again. She continues to trust and aid the contractor, and to wait for "her turn" to come around ... when the contractor will be finished with unknown "*others*" who have been given priority status. She wants to honor her word. After all, she thinks, if she had been able to do the work "right," as expected of her, it wouldn't have had to be corrected or done again and the delays would have been avoided; therefore, it was her fault. She decides to work harder to *do it right* – this time.

Scene 4. A confrontation takes place

The woman, still trusting in the word of the contractor and thinking she has waited patiently long enough, asks him to take his share of the contracted responsibility of finishing the project. He responds, *My other clients are more in "need" than you,* implying, *You want to be the center of the Universe! How can you be so selfish? You want to be "first."*

The Double-Bind

This is the *Double-Bind*; she would be damned if she *didn't* continue to take responsibility for the project and at the same time, she would be damned if she *did* take the responsibility; that is, she would be labeled *"selfish"* if she *didn't* ... (meaning she would be taking *his* valuable time away from *others* who needed him more than she did). She would also be damned if she *did*; that is, she would be labeled *greedy* because she wanted more of "things" than she cared about *others* – meaning she would be *mercenary*, more concerned with her own project than she was with *needy others*; by doing so, she would be making herself "the Center of the Universe" ... putting herself in "first" position. The verdict was "guilty" on both counts, whether she *did* or *didn't* take responsibility. The fact that her agreement was with the contractor and not with unknown *others*, *needy* or otherwise, has been submerged in *unearned* "guilt."

The Reversal

In the Real World, the purchaser's insistence that the contractor fulfill his obligations would merely be that the contractor deliver to her what they had jointly agreed upon. In that respect, she is rightly the center of *her* "universe," not *The* Universe. The contractor reversed roles and *projected* his negative attributes to the purchaser, believing that *he* is the Center of the Universe, as he is the "authority" figure and "controls" the Project. At the same time that he projects his *negative* attributes to the purchaser, he claims her *positive* attributes for himself. He *claims* to be "Good," the *innocent* one, and reverses his "Bad" to her. This is due to the reversal of responsibilities that he overturned by fraud and theft which was followed by a "Guilty" verdict for the purchaser – for not "honoring" *her* "responsibilities," which, as the contractor, were <u>his</u> – but which now, indirectly, he *disowns.*

The position of the purchaser being reversed, she is now caught in a double-bind. She is damned if she claims her original rights according to the agreement, and she is damned if she doesn't, as she would be going against herself. The double-bind is always *for* a *Binder*, in this case, the contractor, and it is always *against* the purchaser, now, the *Bound.*

Fear and Guilt

The *bound* purchaser can perceive that something is terribly wrong, yet not know what is happening. The result is that the Bound may become mentally and emotionally "paralyzed" by the madness of the two impossible propositions, in that each results in inescapable "guilt." The victim is not able to see that the two "choices" she is confronted with are negative choices; in this case, she chose to go against herself and be *for* the Binder-contractor *(obedient)* – in order to be "Good" – to be "unselfish." The fear and guilt of not being nor having *the means* to be good *enough*, now fills her mind and heart.

The Double-Bind is *a Rape of the Mind.*

Scene 5. The Closed System – A New World Order

The Contractor as Guardian-Binder

In accepting to choose for the Binder in Stage 4 the Bound is now entering a New World Order of illogical "logic," an upside-down world. Where formerly her good was good, in this New World it is judged "Bad," and the Binder's bad becomes the "Good." The woman strives harder now to become "Good," and receives *praise* for efforts made to reach her now *continually receding* goal; however, in her efforts she becomes trapped again because *at the same time* that she is "Good," she is also "Bad" – for not reaching the goal as expected of her – for still not doing things "right"; plus, she is "greedy" for pursuing the goal for which she was praised.

However, to be "greedy" becomes the lesser of the two evils because it is "a *necessary* evil," necessary, because the contractor needs to stay in control of the Bound (who is no longer the purchaser) so that she will continue the "work" – which is now *for him* and is "evil" because every action she takes is *polluted* with her Self – she still thinks of the work and the goal as hers – therefore, she is "selfish."   The contractor's solution to this dilemma is to assume the role of *Guardian and Mentor* by admonishing her to continue to *try* to be "good" (obedient) with the *promise* of *praise* as a reward and to try to eliminate her "greed" (selfishness) *by not owning the fruits of her labors, that is, by giving them all to him as his own,* for which she may expect more *praise*.

She is to work and pay for, in advance, with her life and labors, that which has been, and still is, promised, but which she will never receive or own. She is admonished to be *patient* and to *wait* for *her* turn. "*Others*" keep replacing her *earned* position in the queue; she continues to be *praised* as long as she steps back and accepts, in turn, each of the contractor's *"Buts."*

Hope for Herself in the Identification with "Others"

To be "Good" she must, *unknowingly*, keep assuming the role of the "contractor" instead of the purchaser in doing the work he was supposed to do; if she complains, becomes impatient, she is "guilty" of taking him away from "others" *who need him more than she does* and is labeled "*selfish.*" What she is also unaware of is that by becoming "Good" she has become one of the "*others,*" and that she must wait until *all* the "*others*" have been "given" what *they* had contracted for; otherwise, she would be "*selfish.*" The rule is: each "other" must not be first; without exception, *each must step behind an other in order not to be "selfish."* What, in the beginning, was her right to receive, has now become *a promise* of a "*gift*" – to be *given* to her for her obedience in choosing correctly, that is, in "*choosing*" for the Binder and against herself. She has become, *unknowingly*, an "accomplice" to her own demotion *as a supplicant*; he is elevated to the status of the *Benevolent Guardian* of the Bound and of her "*Yes*"-promise "*Gift*" – which will never be reached; it becomes the proverbial carrot on the end of a stick.

The original purchaser/contractor agreement has disappeared by ellipsis.

The Two Faces of the Divided Binder

The Binder alternates between two personalities; one is that of the "*Good Guardian*" who praises (Scene 5); the other is the "*Accuser*" (Scene 6). In Scene 5, he *praises* all his workers, the "others," for their obedience in "choosing correctly." This is easy to do, because there is only one choice that is acceptable. Since all workers now reflect the mind of the Binder, it can be expected that the "right" choice will already have been made in advance. In addition, perfection is still expected, so one must continually try harder, because there is always something else that one has failed to do or that has not been done correctly, for which one receives the label "slothful" and therefore, "guilty." Plus, what you do must not be for yourself, else you would again be "selfish," and likewise, "guilty." The Bound live only for acceptance and praise for their obedience to the Guardian-Binder. They are to *deny* themselves completely; they *blank-out* what they can't understand (the Double-Bind) and enter into a state of *"no-mind"*; they become *de-humanized* and experience an *undefined feeling* of <u>humiliation.</u>

The Binder keeps the Bound continuously in this CLOSED SYSTEM based on a confused "guilty," *emotional-feeling* level which clouds the possibility of questioning and therefore prevents the Bound's ability to reason.

Denial

Conversely, the Real World is an OPEN SYSTEM of individual rationality, creativity, and an expansion of the Self that owns his or her own Identity as *first* person "I." The Binder's reversed world is a CLOSED SYSTEM that repeats incessantly a circular Pattern of Double-Binds. The Binder maintains his newly acquired authority by the continual *Denial* of Reality – by the denial of all <u>pre-existing</u> *facts* of the OPEN SYSTEM. This is the stage of *obfuscation* and *omission*, keeping all followers "asleep" in a state of "forgetfulness" of the original joint agreement, which has been replaced by the Binder's *concealed* goal of *possession* of the Bound and the Bound's possessions. It is as if all events that had happened *before* this New World Order came into being had never existed. All has been reversed and the "history" of the original agreement has been rewritten with the real facts omitted.

The Real World and this fabricated world stand back-to-back, as do the two personalities of the Binder. The new rules are those of the incomprehensible Double-Bind that must never be discovered by the Bound. They must never see that their individuality will no longer exist by its disappearance in being "one" with "others," *all* being of the *same* kind, even in having the same adjectival name "Faithful" bestowed upon them. It is a world of cloned *quantity* instead of unique *quality*.

"Yes – but no – yet is."

A Binder is concerned with *numbers* and must have many followers, many "purchasers," as there are a few who may wake up, begin to question, find answers, and revolt by *standing up*, no longer *suppliant*. There is always the danger that they might leave him; plus, there are others who become incapacitated towards the end of their journey through The Pattern. This is a crucial stage for the Binder; some followers who are not completely "asleep" can begin to remember facts that have been suppressed. In the Real World, human beings, by nature, are curious, and curiosity will always raise its head to question when there is *perceived* to be too great an amount of contradictions. In this case, the "I" begins to *re*-member its individual Self and begins to question the existence of an almost forgotten contract; the Guardian/Binder, becoming fearful of a possible abandonment by his work-force, *kindly* seeks to *rescue* the Bound by reassurances, "What *was*, is *not*, yet *is*." Or, "*Yes*," but, *no*, yet *will be*." In other words, "*Yes*," the promise on the end of the stick is still there, "*But "No,"* *you don't have it* (that is, you just can't *see* it), – "yet, it *will be* obtained sometime in the future, *if* you are *patient* and work hard enough to reach it.

This is another reversal of responsibility ... another Double-Bind:

> If you seek and *do* find, you are "guilty" *(greedy, "selfish")*.

> If you seek and *don't* find, you are "Good" *(patient, "faithful")*.

The insidious nature of this Pattern is that as it progresses, previous stages are used to reinforce a present stage. There is an overlapping where the former becomes *proof of "guilt"* for the later *(as stage 3 is "proof" in stage 6)*.

One Goal

Further, the Bound is reassured by the Binder that *his* goal is *your* goal. Hence, your obedience will be aiding him not only to reach your goal, but the goal of *all* who *also* "*need*" him. You must not think of yourself in the aspect of *First Person*; your goal is the same as for all of *us;* you must help *us* ... to obtain *our* goal.

One Size Fits All

It is a reminder that you must not be the *speaker*, the center of your own universe. From being the singular *First Person* "*I*," the Bound person becomes one of many in the plural, objective, accusative case "*us*." The Bound becomes part of the *Corporate Body Politic* "*We*," as against the Individual *Corporeal* "*I*." The Binder holds all plans in his own hands; his plans are your plans and vice versa. This Architect personality is the "*Guardian*" ... you are *all* safe in his hands; there is *safety* in *numbers* – you *must not* be *singled* out. The *single individual* becomes an outcast in dangerous territory and *is the exception to the rule that there is only One mind for All.*

Scene 6. The Other Face of the Binder – The Accuser

The woman still has not completely forgotten the original contract; the memory keeps surfacing unsolicited, and with it the humiliation of being "guilty" for this *lack of "self" control*, of not being able to keep the "agreement" submerged. (Another Double-Bind: she has been *deprived of Self* by the Binder, and then is *blamed for not having* a *Self, that is,* "*Self-control*.") However, when the pain of repression, the emotional and intellectual stagnation gets too great, she musters the courage *to speak* to the "contractor." She complains that she is required to do too much of the work, and has not received from him what he had contracted to do. At this point, the Binder becomes very *angry* and *accuses* her, "*It is not I, but you, who are to blame; you chose to do the work (in stage 3); it is not my honor that is at stake; it is your honor.*" Here, she is punished for being punished; that is, she did not *choose* to be the purchaser *and* the contractor. That was fraudulently accomplished, which was the first punishment. The second punishment was of being "guilty" for not "honoring" a fraudulent agreement. Again, the facts were turned upside-down, *her own perceptions invalidated.*

The Accuser/Guardian

In this New World Order, only her dependence on and obedience to the Binder can now fulfill her longings. A depression sets in – she is always "guilty" ... *she can never please* the Binder. She cannot see the results of her work to her benefit; the work she continues to do suffers as a consequence; she is then *demonized* ... accused of being *"perverse."* Perversity cannot be tolerated; if the *Accuser's* words of *intimidation and threats* do not *coerce her to trust* and to continue her obedience to him, then physical force may be applied by the *Accuser/Enforcer-Guardian.*

Scene 7. The Guardian/Enforcer

The Binder in this stage, to obtain submission, may use threats or intimidation, and if these should fail may resort to physical force. As the *Accuser/Enforcer*, the Binder has a compulsion to punish the Bound for her "disobedience" for questioning <u>his</u> "honor." Her *defense* and *assertion* to confirm the original joint agreement is condemned as *"aggression."* He threatens to withdraw the *"promise"* entirely – if she doesn't *trust* him. He is, in this way, accusing her of not being *able* to trust when he asks *What's the matter, don't you <u>trust</u> me?* A reversal has taken place; *in accusing her,* <u>he is the aggressor</u> (the Enforcer) *and at the same time* <u>he is the "defender"</u> of his *"claim" that he is trustworthy* (the Guardian).

This dual personality creates a *Double-Bind* by projection; if she says *"No,* I *don't* trust you" – she goes against the Binder and therefore, *becomes* the *"aggressor";* plus, she will be "guilty" for not being *able* to *trust.* (At this point, the Binder may become very angry and resort to physical violence.) If she says *"Yes,* I *do* trust you" – she goes against herself and loses her factual defense and her goals.

He "gains"; she loses. Whichever way the coin lands, "Heads" or "Tails," he *always* "wins" – *he thinks.* As will be seen, the more he "wins," the more he loses ... the snake eats his own tail.

Don't See this as Punishment

In this stage, as Guardian, he says, *Don't see this as punishment; I do this for your own good*; that is, *see* punishment as "Good." The punishment is *justified* by the "reasons" given by the *Accuser* in Stage 6, when he reversed reality by the accusation, *"I, not you, am 'Good,'"* or *"You, not I, are 'Bad.'"* *"You can't be trusted to honor your word."* As the *Guardian*, he says (1) *"Punishing you hurts me more than it does you."* (2) *"I punish you because I love you."* Here, the Guardian and the Enforcer merge into One.

Black is "White"

Punishment becomes "love"; *Black becomes "White."* The *words* of "love" remind the Bound of the Binder's promises; she again feels guilty because she has "failed" – again. She believes she was the sole cause of her having to be punished. *The Binder really cares for me and my goals* she thinks, ... and then "repents" of her "wrong doing." She feels *shame* for having been so "insensitive," "*unable* to trust," and for being "aggressive." This is the stage of *submission* to the Binder, *the rape of the Bound's emotions which have been reversed to the Binder's projection of the feelings he needs her to have in order to continue the "binding."* It defines the Binder's *compulsion to punish*; in punishing, he is the *Accuser/Enforcer* which then allows him to be the *"comforter,"* the *Guardian-Healer* who restores *"peace."* The Binder *causes* the Bound to be *"evil,"* punishes the Bound for *being* "evil," then steps in to become the "Comforter" who "forgives" upon the Bound's confession of "guilt." After all, if the Bound had been completely obedient punishment would not have been necessary; therefore, the Bound *"asked for it."*

This stage is a recurring vortex that sends the Bound down into a deep depression.

The Law of Diminishing Returns

The Bound *must* obey, and fraud and force are the means the Binder uses to bind them both together as *One*. The Binder can only exist by thieving from the Bound. This however, unknowingly, creates a loss to himself by the eroding Law of Diminishing Returns. The more he takes of the Selves of others for nourishment, the less of his own capacity for Self-nourishment remains. The Binder becomes empty at this stage, as he now "feeds" on *non*-selves – the Bound person has very little Self left to "give." As a result, she flows through him like water through a sieve, which creates an abyss in the Binder that becomes filled with compulsions, a constant hunger and thirst that cannot be satisfied nor quenched. The Binder then "beats a dead horse" when he punishes the Bound for "withholding" from him what she can no longer "give."

Scene 8. "Voluntary" Union – Love/Hate

Here, the Binder and the Bound have become *One* in a "voluntary" union; *"voluntary,"* because she has "chosen" without choosing. The woman no longer has thoughts or emotions of her own; dead to her Self, she has become dumb to the former and numb to the latter. She no longer lives as a human being in the Real World. In each stage, the Bound's own perceptions and emotions have been invalidated, *trapped in a cul-de-sac*, which effectively walls off the ability to reason. The Binder, as the *Enforcer*, has killed what he, as the *Guardian*, professed to love, then asks, *Where is love for me?* The Binder, as *Guardian*, wants his cake and, as the *Enforcer*, to eat it, too. This is the essence of the Love/Hate syndrome, which leads to stage 9.

Scene 9. Depression – Psychological Cannibalism

Extreme depression and withdrawal ensues for both the Binder and the Bound. The Bound has been emptied and has no more to give, leaving the Binder without the nourishment that had sustained him. If this state is not checked, suicide, or murder/suicide could follow. Binder-expressed, this is *"If I can't have it, you can't have it."* – the result of both being Bound together in death as well as in life. Life/Death and Love/Hate merge into one, becoming synonymous – Love is Life and Hate is Death – Hatred of the Self kills Love, and this Death kills Life ... psychologically ... or physically.

This whole process could be defined as *"Psychological Cannibalism."*

*　　*　　*

*"He who would gather immortal palms must not be hindered by the **name** of goodness, but must explore if it be goodness. Nothing is at last sacred but the integrity of your own mind.*

~ *Ralph Waldo Emerson, "Self-Reliance"*

MASTER CHART
Description of Stages in the Pattern

	STAGE-EVENT	EMOTIONS	FUNCTION	DESCRIPTION
1	Problem	Anxiety	Question	Fear
2	Agreement	Trust	Solution	Safety
3	Identity Crisis	Confusion	Mind-Bind	Ambiguity "Yes, but...."
4	Reversal	Guilt/Fear	Rape of Mind	Double-Bind: Damned if do. Damned if don't.
5	Denial	Humiliation	Blank-out; No-Mind	Dehumanized: "Yes, but no, yet is."
6	Accusation	Guilt/Shame	Binder projects his guilt.	Demonized: "Not I, but you..."
7	Punishment	Helplessness Depression	Compulsion – Subjection	Punished for being punished. "See black as white."
8	Bound	Love/Hate	Brain-washed	"Voluntary" Union
9	Death/Suicide	Numb Death of feelings.	Dumb Death of the mind.	Psychological Cannibalism.

Part II

The Pattern of The Double-Bind in Mormonism

In the fall of 1997, my son, Matt, and I discovered Eric Kettunen's Internet site, *Recovery from Mormonism.* Until that time, we thought that we were alone in our discoveries about Mormonism and in leaving the church. As I read each Post, I was impressed with the similarities of personal experiences ... and how they coincided with my own. I could see aspects of The Pattern in each Post and some explicitly contained most, if not all, aspects. They filled in, and clarified more fully the stages of this Pattern in Mormonism for me.

Stage 1: Problem – Anxiety
Question – Fear

How The Pattern is Used in Mormonism
The Closed System

Basic Survival Needs

This first stage concerns Human Relationships and *Life*. A *problem* exists, something is missing, and this void makes our lives feel empty, or incomplete ... we can even feel as if our very survival is threatened. Its core is centered on our closest ties to reality – the *family*.

Unsatisfied longings urge us to seek fulfillment so that we can feel complete. This lack becomes a problem because we cannot function well until the problem is solved; in some cases, we may even become incapacitated emotionally and mentally. We look for solutions and are vulnerable in our search because we are going into unknown territory; we have no previous experience to guide us. We seek out those who seem to know or have answers ... those who can help us fill the void.

Whether one is born into Mormonism, or not, everyone's need is for *genuine*, human social relationships ... *personal*, sympathetic, caring relationships ... to be understood – to love and to be loved. These are *human* needs that are acknowledged in the *Open System* of reality. We are *individuals* with *social* needs. If these needs are missing, a void is created. Between each stage of the maturation process, there is a transitional stage of relative confusion. Ideally, to reach the next stage of growth we will have been previously taught problem-*solving* principles, in general, in order to apply them to a present confusion. Ironically, this is not applied nor taught in the realm of family relationships within Mormonism, even though its doctrinal base is the family. The *words* may be spoken, but the *means* are omitted.

Every problem has a personal or social element in it, and as a result, our feelings or our perceptions of a conflict can cloud, temporarily, our ability to think clearly. Those with experience know that it is always best not to make long range serious decisions while under the sway of confused emotions. They have been made aware of this pitfall and *expect* the confusion that arises out of this *potentially* positive *growth* process. Just like the "growing pains" we experienced in our bones as children, we experience mental and emotional "growing pains." But, if we have not been made aware of this normal process, we are extremely vulnerable to answers given us from any source that promises to relieve the pain we are experiencing ... anything that will fill the void. In that case, we depend on our pain or pleasure impulses; whatever "sounds" like the answer we need and makes us *feel* better is "good"; what doesn't instantly make us feel good is "bad."

What is bypassed is the reasoning process which would allow us to be able to see the "fine print," the *"Buts"* of a contract, and where it *all* may lead. We use this same reasoning process when we buy a used car or a house. The emotions are still there but are grounded in reasonable reality. This applies to the most important decisions we make in this life; it is mentally and emotionally satisfying to *know* what we are buying, and that we have chosen it rationally, with confidence. This is the real world of choice in the *Open System.* *There can be no real choice without this knowledge.* The *Closed System* of Mormonism gives "lip service" to reality, then negates it by keeping its members in an emotional, and rationally confused state of mind from which they "choose ... without choosing"; they "choose" the *label* that best fits their needs without being shown the contents.

The following examples of the first stage, *A Problem*, show how it applies to new converts – how they *chose* Mormonism. For the majority of Mormons born into the church their *choice* had already been made for them.

I will list only the Post number after each excerpt. In some cases, you can follow the same Post through other stages, thereby seeing The Pattern as it evolved with that particular person. The Posts themselves can be read in full on Eric's *Freedom from Mormonism* Web Site (formerly *Recovery from Mormonism).*

Personal Experiences

Stage 1 A Problem – Anxiety

Posts by Women Converts to Mormonism

"I joined the LDS church at the age of 14 through the urging of a high school friend. ... I was not very popular in school, but among the LDS youth I found an instant kinship."   Post #3

"I joined the church at age 8 with my family. My parents were trying to salvage their marriage and they thought that perhaps the church might help them. Unfortunately, they were beyond help and eventually divorced. Over a period of time, all my family members stopped going except me. I found acceptance at church and as

long as I could get a ride, my mother let me keep attending."
Post # 9

"I was raised Methodist in rural North Carolina, but always felt
something was missing from my life. ... I ... became even more
attracted to the Mormon lifestyle. I wanted that sense of security
that comes from a church that can answer all your questions
(there's an explanation for EVERYTHING) and tells you what's
right or wrong so you don't have to think for yourself. As an
adolescent about to turn 17, desperately trying to fit in somewhere,
life was confusing and scary, and I needed that guidance."   Post
#13

"I was being harassed by my 'ex-husband' and feeling glad to be
out of my home on Sundays, in a place where my ex-husband
would not be able to find me. At that point, my intentions were only
to continue to visit the church."   Post #16

"I was nineteen and a nursing student in Canada when I joined the
church. I wonder how many converts join the Mormon Church
because they are in a vulnerable position when they meet the
missionaries or a member of the church. I grew up as a Ward of
the Children's Aid Society and lived in a foster home. I
experienced a lot of ridicule from other children and adults who
called me 'illegitimate orphan.' ... So the timing was right for me
when I met the missionaries who were teaching that God loves all
of us."   Post #37

"When I was 21, I met a young man who befriended and comforted
me after my Dad's passing, and while my Mom was dying. I was
EXTREMELY vulnerable at that time as I felt my whole world was
being erased. He and his family took me in, and made me feel
that they would always be there for me..."   Post # 32 – 2

"I was 12 years old and we were living in Council Bluffs, IA when my parents were divorced. Shortly thereafter my older brother, my sister, and I had the missionary discussions. My father still refused to give us permission to be baptized, but our stake president said we could go ahead in order that my older brother who was only 14, could receive the priesthood so that our home would have the priesthood in it. We were trebly marginalized; being a divorced family, poor, and not from Utah, we were on the fringe of the ward." Post #43

"I grew up in Orange County, California and as a young child, I was burdened by the ongoing family problems of my home. The fighting between my parents at one point became so bad, plus the fighting between my older brother & my father (his step-dad), that I can remember going through severe depression & wanting desperately to die. Life had no meaning or purpose & I didn't think I could be strong enough emotionally to endure home life." Post #48

"My marriage wasn't going so well and we lived in Puerto Rico at that time so I was a long way from my family. Well guess who knocked on my door one day???? Right!!! Two fine looking young men in white shirts and ties." Post #53

"During the initial period of my separation and divorce, I turned in desperation to the Bible for some type of guidance, because I was scared about being a single mother and was unsure as how much strength (psychologically) I had. It was right about this time that the missionaries came to my door." Post #54

"As I look back now I know I was vulnerable to the church's message. The wholesomeness, family togetherness and built-in social life were all things I wanted to be part of." Post #68

Posts by Men Converts to Mormonism

"I grew up in the stereotypical 'dysfunctional' family. My father was an alcoholic. My mother divorced him in my teens. I lost one of my younger brothers in an accident at an early age. ... Basically, I was a sitting duck for Mormonism, or 'golden' as the missionaries would say." Post #28 – 1

"After finishing college I married an inactive Utah girl and moved to a very small rural Mormon community. At first we felt kind of lonely and isolated. The local towns folk made the initial feelers regarding our interest with their LDS church. By not rejecting the fellowship and inquiries of these members my wife and I were giving them passive approval to continue their activity. Soon the flood gates opened. The more we embraced the local ward, the more the doting church members went out of their way to make us feel right at home. It seemed that the whole town had an interest in our welfare. My older brother showed up for a few days and assisted the local members with their missionary efforts. I was baptized soon after. We bought a beautiful little home. Life was good in our corner of the world. In a way I was taking the path of least resistance. ... Sometimes it is not always clear when this is a good idea." Post #47

"One of the common threads I have observed in this group is the vulnerability within ourselves, converts, when we are looking for a church to join. I was extremely vulnerable with trying to hold my marriage together, and dealing with the moral guilt of having participated in a war. It (war) was a time when many of us lost our innocence, and how fantastic it felt to be baptized and forgiven, but it was only an illusion. That experience of reality/illusion is something we all shared when we were members of the LDS Church. It is a fantastic feeling to be a part of this forum, and to finally experience reality." Post #49

Posts by Couples Converted to Mormonism

"We had a terrible experience when our oldest daughter was five and our youngest three. ... Our little five year old was killed instantly by a falling beam. My wife and I were devastated. Our world turned up side down. My wife was in such shock that she had to be sedated for several days. I was numb all over. Remember, neither my wife nor I had had any religious training in our childhood. So for us this was the end of our little girl."   Post # 25

"... I was getting homesick for California and after having my first child I felt like I needed my family. So I guess the church was the closest thing to that."   Post #33

Stages 2 – 3: Agreement – Identity Crisis

The *problem* in Stage 1 created a need for answers ... the Where, How, Why and When of a solution. It is in this mental and emotional confusion that Mormonism steps in with a formula that "fits all problems." This it does in Stage 2 and 3.

Agreement

The *Milk* Agreement – The "Yes" – Trust – Safety

Stage 2 In Mormonism the key factor is an agreement based on hidden facts, in short, a fraudulent contract. This *black* contract has a *white* label *"Yes"* attached to it, which is called *milk*. A member of the church, however, is never allowed to be weaned from *milk*. What they call the *meat* of its doctrine is hidden below the *milk* which sinks deeper and deeper the more the member seeks to reach it. Without realizing it, the member *is* the meat ... that is being *eaten*; the individual's human Identity will eventually be absorbed piece-meal within the vast body of Mormonism. The first *bite* is taken in Stage 3.

Identity Crisis

"Yes, ... But ..." – "If ..." – Ambiguity – Confusion

Stage 3 New members are caught with a psychological hook. It begins with the *"Yes"* agreement, which is then altered by a *pre*-positional *"But,"* this is what you must do ... *extra*; the *extra* is part of the hidden *meat* contained in the agreement, which is now being demoted to an ambiguous *promise* ... with hidden strings of expectation and hope, instead of concrete assurance. The roles between the purchaser and the contractor are beginning to be reversed. The member is no longer the purchaser granted the rights of an agreement, but is becoming a supplicant who must say *please,* to which the Binder says, *"Yes,"* if you do more work – to become *worthy* to receive. This is a further demotion of *what* is to be *received*; instead of the concrete agreement, it has now subtly been changed into a *promise.* What is now to be received is a *"gift" given, "If"* ... you become *worthy* to receive. A definite agreement has become an *undefined* worthiness in order to receive.

Unknown to you as a new member, in order to become *worthy,* eventually, you must take an oath that *all* you own, including yourself, belongs to the Church; this is the hidden part of the *meat* of the original contract. Once received, the Church *promises* to give back to you, as a *gift,* that which you had formerly owned ... if you become *worthy* ... at some point in the unknown *future.*

This is a critical stage; it is the wedge that opens the door to a final *"voluntary"* loss of Identity. It begins with an insertion into the agreement of a *"But."*

Stages 2 – 3   Agreement / *Promise* – Ambiguity

Posts by Women – Stages 2 – 3

The Promise

"My husband and I visited the ward patriarch. ... His blessing told of the many wondrous things he was to take part in and accomplish 'HERE UPON THE EARTH.'"

Ambiguity

"Eight months after that, my husband was diagnosed with inoperable brain cancer. ... the first thing church elders tried to do when I brought up the question of why this promise was given then not fulfilled was to say (*"Yes, but"*) 'perhaps the blessing speaks of his duties in the Spirit World.'" Post #3 *See: Stage 1, #3*

*   *

The Promise – *("Yes")*

> Moroni's promise of the manifestation of the Holy Ghost, the "burning in the bosom."

Ambiguity – *("But")*

"I had never received a burning of the bosom or anything despite much prayer and study. ... Since I could never seem to achieve Moroni's promise of the burning in my bosom, I thought something was wrong with me and that God didn't love me anymore. I secretly thought that perhaps I had done something so horrible, God had already relegated me to outer darkness. *(She was told)* ... that serving as relief society president would help my testimony grow stronger." Post # 9 *See: Stage 1, #9*

*   *

Agreement

"I gave in, as they re-assured me that the content of the lessons was 'all that is needed for baptism.'"

(The "Yes" ... to the "milk.")

Identity crisis – Reversal

("But") "I was to soon find out that their theology was to be revealed in small installments, perhaps to make it digestible, and that all the priesthood holders believed they had authority over me." Post #16 *See: Stage 1, #16*

> *The original agreement was gradually being modified, as well as the roles. Instead of being the "chooser," she was becoming the "chosen" by those who now claimed to have*

authority over her. The hidden "meat" is revealed only piece-meal.

*   *

Agreement – *To listen*

"However, I had the six discussions over and over again and argued all the way to my baptism. I joined the church for two reasons ... *(one of which was)* as an insurance policy. When the missionaries taught about people being taught the gospel on the other side after they died I told them that I would wait and join the church on the other side rather than join now."

(She had been given the "milk" promise.)

Ambiguity – Confusion

"They told me that since they had already taught me the gospel I would never have another chance to hear it and therefore would not get to heaven. I was afraid not to join; I felt trapped. Now I call it manipulation."   Post #37 *See: Stage 1, #37*

This is the "Yes," then the "but" as the hidden "meat" after the fact. The "but" in translation means "No." This is also a double-bind. Damned if she did wait (intimidation from and against the Binder), and damned if she didn't wait (it would be against her Self).

*   *

The Promise

"I told the missionaries I followed the instructions of Moroni as suggested in Moroni 10:3 – 5 but I did not receive an answer one way or the other."

Ambiguity

("Yes," she tried, "but" ...) "They told me I needed to pray more and to be sincere. I felt embarrassed that they were telling me I was not sincere in my prayers because the Book of Mormon was

true and I could know. I prayed some more and still nothing."
Post #37 *See: Stage 1, #37*

*   *

The Promise

"... wearing the garments made me feel special and just a cut above people who weren't 'worthy' to wear them. I felt protected from the sins of the world and Satan." (*"Yes"*)

Ambiguity

(*"But"*) "I was always struggling with some sin or other though and always felt 'unworthy'. I can't remember a time when I really felt that I was living up to the standards and expectations of the church."   Post # 53 *See: Stage 1, #53*

*   *

The Promise #1

"The following January 1, I received my patriarchal blessings and was overwhelmed by the promises. Wow, it even said that my mother was very much aware of what I had been doing, and she had accepted the gospel in the spirit world..." (*"Yes ..."*)

Ambiguity

(... *"But"*) " ... waited upon me to do her work here."

The Promise #2 *("Yes")*

"While in the mission home, we were able to attend another temple session and then be addressed by Pres. Harold B. Lee in the Solemn Assembly Room in the temple. We had a question and answer session with Pres. Lee."

Ambiguity *("But")*

"Being shy, I felt doubly intimidated when we were admonished that since Pres. Lee was giving up time in his busy schedule to be there that our questions needed to be important enough for him to spend his time on. Well, either many others were scared also or they already knew it all because there were not many questions asked during that session." Post #68 *See: Stage 1, #68*

> *"Yes, but ... don't." Don't be "selfish"; there are others who need him more than you do.*

*   *

The Promise (This is one of the most common "Yes, Buts.")

Book of Mormon, Moroni 10:4

("Yes.") And when ye receive these things, I would exhort you that ye would ask God, the Eternal Father, in the name of Christ, if these things are *not* true; and if ye shall ask with a sincere heart, with real intent, having faith in Christ, he will manifest the truth of it unto you, by the power of the Holy Ghost.

> *(The word "manifest" means (1) readily perceived by the senses and esp. by the sight (2) easily understood or recognized by the mind: obvious syn evident.* Webster's Dictionary. Italics, mine.)

"It got to the point where just reading the BoM again for the required religion class made me sit in the middle of my bed and cry because I kept thinking, 'I've read this on Sundays, I've read this in Seminary, I'm reading this now, I'll read parts of it again this Sunday, and hear parts at endless firesides and meetings until doomsday, ...

Ambiguity

... but WHERE IS MY TESTIMONY!!!'" I'd said I'd had one for years, said the same to get into BYU, but I didn't. I wanted one, but the Spirit never visited me. I followed all the rules and read that little book endless times, but I never got any burning anywhere." Post #69

> *Note: The* reason *given for the failure to receive the* manifestation *is always something the suppliant has failed to comply with. It says "Yes," you can receive confirmation*

"But," *somehow you didn't do something right; try again. This is a subtle reversal of claimed responsibility and roles. Instead of the leaders of the church with the supposed* manifestation *of the "spirit"* knowing *that the supplicant was sincere, they obscure the facts and blame the supplicant. They find a "red herring," a chastisement ... a "flaw," that obscures the supplicant's innocence, and instills more feelings of unworthiness, guilt, failure and fear.*

Posts by Men – Stages 2 – 3

The Promise – Of the Spirit

"Religious instruction starts early with constant reinforcement. Everyone around me was so sure Mormonism was the right religion."

Identity Crisis

"I felt that I was just a bad person who wasn't getting it. These feelings continued to grow as I did. I tried to believe. I read the Book of Mormon and prayed about it. I never received the 'burning in the bosom' talked about by Mormons. This was supposed to be a signal from God that the individual had found the true Church. This made me feel even worse."   Post #2

*   *

The Promise

(An impossible promise begets an impossible compliance in the real world.)

Ambiguity – Mind-Bind – Identity Crisis

"I view the years I spent as a Mormon as a kind of mindrape. Mormonism gave me a terrible self-image (I could not live up to the impossible, 'perfect' expectations) that I am only recently recovering from."   Post #10

*   *

The Promise

"I never sought proof that the Mormon church was true, and for the first 23 years of my life, I tried with all of my heart to believe. To the reader who might say that I simply did not have the faith, or that my faith was not true, I have this as an answer: Since my ambiguous feelings about the church have always been with me, does that mean I was faithless as a child? And if so, where does that leave the teachings of your god in regards to little children? Throughout my life I wanted it to be true, I hoped it would be true, ... (*"Yes"*)

Identity Crisis – Ambiguity

... **but** the promises made by my teachers, church leaders, parents, and general authorities were all empty as far as they related to my own life." Post #19

*   *

The Promise

"So I told him *(the bishop)* that, although I had never had that feeling that somehow I had always known it was true. What I was really saying was that I had always accepted that it was true, for no other reason than I had always been taught that it was true and that I couldn't conceive of such a large organization being false and nobody in the Mormon church knowing about it. ... I'd stood up in Testimony meetings and borne 'my' testimony, hoping that somehow I'd get one – always having been told that bearing your testimony made it stronger –

Ambiguity

– but I never did." Post #21

*   *

The Promise

"... I was escorted to a chair in front of the assembled congregation for the 'laying on of hands'; the part in which newly baptized

Mormons receive the Holy Spirit. Previously, I was told by many of the missionaries that I would feel a 'burning in my bosom.' A 'baptism of fire.' ... The missionaries made it clear to me that I would actually feel the Holy Spirit enter my body. They wanted to prepare me for what to expect."

Ambiguity

"It was during the laying on of hands that I first noticed an emptiness in my new religion. I felt nothing. I cried in anticipation of an overwhelming experience of a holy being entering my newly cleansed body, but as hands were placed on my head, I felt absolutely nothing. 'Here it comes ... here it comes ...' Then suddenly the prayer ended, the hands were removed, and there I sat with a big line of snot hanging from my chin. NOTHING. Where was the cymbal crash? Where was the Holy Spirit? ... Afterwards, I told some of the missionaries about what had happened during the 'laying on of hands.' ... I then was told that the Holy Spirit sometimes manifests himself in a gentle, quiet way, and that this peaceful silence is certainly much more beautiful than any kind of burning in my bosom, or any other 'sign' or 'feeling' from God. Besides, 'signs,' they said, are not necessary for true believers. Since I was truly converted, I didn't need a trumpet blast. I was even told that during the 'laying on of hands' the Holy Spirit does not necessarily enter one's body at that time, but may enter only when necessary. That sounded odd to me. After all, '... receive the Holy Spirit ...' was said during the blessing. ... I was even told that though I might not feel the Holy Spirit enter my body, I will certainly feel it leave when I commit sin. (Does anyone sense a cult tactic here?) This was a blatant flip-flop by the missionaries. ... But, I wanted to believe it. I had come so far and wanted to believe so much. I accepted their explanation."   Post # 28 – 2
See: Stage 1, #28 – 1

*   *

Promise #1

"I had been taught those who prayed sincerely and in righteousness would receive a testimony ...

Ambiguity

"... and if they did not, one chief reason would be that they were not recognizing the answer God was giving. ... I had been praying to know whether or not the Church was true ... I continued to pray, but God said nothing to me ..."

Promise #2

"Prior to my mission, I had been given blessings by Brad Thompson ... prophecies were given to me of great success that I would have as a missionary. ... He said I would have such success that other missionaries would see it and come to me to learn how to copy it."

Ambiguity

"... I put my heart into seeing these prophecies fulfilled, but they were not. ... At this time, it seemed to me that if I earnestly desired these blessings, that I would weep about my not having received them. So I began to weep much during the last year or so of my mission. For prayer, I would weep about God's not talking to me. As I wept to hear God's voice, Brad continued to prophesy blessings upon my mission. Yet, none of these prophecies were fulfilled. ... Brad ... gave several different possible explanations: 1) the prophecies would suddenly, dramatically be fulfilled in the last few months or weeks of my mission, 2) the prophecies were fulfilled, but I did not perceive it, 3) I had planted many seeds in many hearts, fulfilling the prophecies, 4) the prophecies would yet be fulfilled, & 5) he may have added to the prophecies out of his own mind. ... None of Brad's prophecies were fulfilled."

"After I left the LDS Church, I have told my story to other LDS. Generally, I do not get far before they are explaining to me my spiritual mistakes. My various spiritual mistakes, according to them, run as follows, though each LDS has a slightly different list:

1) it was your first mistake to pray for angels to teach you, when you had bishops and other church leaders to teach you;

2) it was a mistake to give much credence to Brad, George Pace and Chauncey Riddle, if at any point they taught ideas not taught

by the general authorities. Since each of them taught 'strange doctrines,' you should have disregarded their teachings;

3) it was a mistake to believe that an elders' quorum president could prophesy about your life in matters outside his jurisdiction as EQ president, specifically, about your mission and the rest of your life;

4) it was a mistake to insist about being absolutely certain about whether or not the Church is true, when in fact, one must have some degree of faith;

5) it was a mistake to believe, based on Brad's teachings, that God might give you doctrinal information He had not given a priesthood leader of yours.

6) it was a mistake to believe that God would use you in a special way, above the way he was using your priesthood leaders.

7) it was a mistake to not know and believe that God honors His priesthood authority, by His telling His prophets, and by extension, all priesthood leaders, all that would be helpful. Thus, there was no need for me to expect any special revelation from God to me during my mission. There was, in fact, no further need of God to speak to me even after my mission, about doctrinal matters. My sole duty was to believe and obey what He had already revealed in and through the LDS Church."

"Further, some suggest that I was emotionally ill. There is no doubt that I was. The only question is what was the cause and the exact nature of my 'mental illness.' They suggest that, in a mild form, I was suffering delusions of grandeur, caused by my close association with that other fellow, Brad Thompson, who happened to be my EQ president when I first came to BYU. He also, in his own way, suffered delusions of grandeur. In a way, this suggestion is no doubt true. The only question is as to whether Mormonism itself feeds such delusions."

(This also contains a Double-Bind; see Stage 4, #38.)

"In any case, there is a short answer to the charge that I made a series of spiritual mistakes that led me out of the LDS Church. The patriarch, in my patriarchal blessing, had promised, 'When you serve your mission, you will have a correct understanding of the gospel.' When I served my mission, I believed in full form, or in seed form, all the spiritual errors that the LDS later held to be responsible, first for my spiritual despair in l981, and later, for my leaving the LDS Church in 1985. The only matter left unknown in 1981, was how my 'spiritual errors' would resolve themselves." Post #38

*   *

Promise

"... I had questions, specifically regarding Joseph Smith and the spirit world; pre- and after. I was told, 'if this part is true, and you believe it, then the rest of it will come to you in the future. Just have faith, and it will be "born" to you.'"

Ambiguity

"Somewhere in here, the Seventies told stories of people who went their entire lives before they learned the completeness of the gospel. All I had to do was be patient. The Seventies were mature men and seemed very credible."   Post #49 *See: Stage 1, #49*

*   *

Promise: If he prayed, his doubts about the church would disappear.

"Towards the beginning of this search I had a temple recommend interview with a member of my ward bishopric. ... I frankly discussed my feelings regarding the church. ... I explained that I had prayed and fasted regarding these issues. ...

Ambiguity – Identity Crisis

" ... (I) still felt that God was telling me that certain doctrines were incorrect. He simply told me that I needed to pray about it more. ... So, I guess my question is, why should a Mormon even bother to pray? They already have all the answers in the handy dandy lesson books. And if you should choose to pray about an issue, and find that your answer is not in line with what the church teaches, you can rest assured that it is you who are wrong. And that your answer was from Satan and not from God. So again I

ask, WHY BOTHER TO PRAY ABOUT ANYTHING???
Remember ... 'when the brethren speak the thinking has been
done.'" Post #58

*   *

Promise

"But, I can't ignore those gnawing questions in my gut. When I
start to think about them I (at least) start to feel some peace about
being true to myself. Is that the spirit talking to me?"

Ambiguity

"The spirit of the devil masquerading as an angel of light some
would say. God is trying my faith others would say. I'm sick of
those pat criticisms that aim to discredit the validity of what I am
feeling." Post #62

*   *

Promise

"Patriarchal Blessings: My mother makes a big deal out of
patriarchal blessings – especially the blessings of family members
that seem to be so insightful and prophetic of great works to come.
Maybe it was my own spectacular blessing that got her on the kick.

Ambiguity

"I, however, grew uncomfortable with the subject. I couldn't help
but ask myself, What if these things don't happen? Nobody in the
church believes that if their blessing says they will live to do some
great work, that they are guaranteed to live long enough to achieve
it. Sure it is God's own promise to you, but you could still get hit by
a bus next week. So how do we faithful members explain that?
There are a whole heap of excuses that try to let God keep his
integrity, but when you add them all up the blessing is unreliable,
even meaningless. Try these on for size:

"The blessings' promises will be fulfilled in the spirit world.

"We just misinterpreted the blessing – Gods ways are not our ways.

"The recipient of the blessing was a sinner, so God took back his promises.

"These loopholes, when combined with the inherent vagueness of the patriarchal blessing, are enough to explain away any discrepancy. And usually, with retrospect and faith, you can dream up some kind of correlation between the blessing and real events – enough to keep or even build your faith. Astrologers and palm readers rely on the same things: vagueness, built-in excuses, and faith of the recipient – plus, the patriarch gets an intimate interview with the subject and is very familiar with the LDS background that has shaped the subject's life."   Post #63

Stage 4: Reversal – Double-Bind

If Stage 3 of The Pattern is the wedge into the brain, Stage 4 shatters it into two opposite sides, severing connections ... the very functions that are necessary for the reasoning process.

THE MAZE OF MORMONISM

Guilt/Fear – Rape of Mind

This stage is built upon stages 2 and 3. A promise was made and then not fulfilled. A "but" was then inserted as the reason for not receiving what was promised. The "but" excuse then becomes a replacement for the promise; something was not done "right" by the would-be recipient who is now blamed for not being *able* to receive. Obedience to the "but" is now required to become *worthy* to receive.

Stage 4 The Double-Bind – "Guilty, Guilty"

"You are damned if you *do* a thing," and "You are damned if you *don't* do it."

One classic Double-Bind in Mormonism involves receiving the "burning in the bosom," the manifestation of the Holy Ghost, as a requirement for a testimony and sanctification. The promise is that *if* you pray *sincerely* you will receive a "burning in the bosom," which is the *manifestation* that the Book of Mormon is true. If you don't receive a "burning in the bosom," you were not "sincere," or there are other things you must do to be "worthy" of receiving it. This is the "Yes, but" stage; "Yes, you prayed, but ..." The "but" then, becomes the focal point, the "hook." It becomes "the carrot on the end of a stick" that can never be reached and becomes the means for your being judged "guilty" for your inability to work hard enough to "get it." This leads into the blatant Double-Bind, which says:

> **If you *don't* obey the "But-things," you will be "guilty" of not being "sincere," not trying hard enough.**
>
> **If you *do* obey the "But-things," you are "guilty" because you still haven't received the "burning in the bosom," which you would have received had you done them properly.**

At this point many other suggestions are given to help you "earn," through work, what was promised you if you were only "sincere" and had worked hard enough. You now need "help" in order to prepare yourself to be made "worthy" of receiving this "gift." More "buts" are issued, as "helps," and the fact that you seem to be outnumbered makes you feel that "I am the only one who doesn't get it" ... you think that "if I work hard enough I will not be the only one who can't 'get it.'" The truth is, the many others, also, "don't get it" – that is, they have been caught in the same maze. The irony is that the ones who "can't get it" are the ones who *are* sincere, and authentic ... the ones who are earnestly trying to keep the integrity of their own minds. (*See Post #19 below.*)

This leads to another Dilemma:

We are told we must live by *faith* alone, in a *non*-physical, that is, a non-brain, non-rational, mental state. *At the same time,* we are told that the *sign* of the *physical* "burning in the bosom" is *proof* of the Book of Mormon, the *necessary* confirmation of its being true. The irony is in the reverse. A *legitimate* burning in the bosom only happens in the real world as an extension of a true, *physical* brain-perception leading to a rational result ... making neural connections! It does not occur when our *individual* perceptions and our brain are *not* involved. The pseudo opposite of this would be the "warm, fuzzy" feeling one gets without mental effort – a longing to belong – to be "one" with all the *others* who *know* ... in order to be "good"; truth is the result of a *rational struggle*, not the longing submission to warm suggestions. It is not the blind acceptance of the Binder's projected upside-down "Good." It is a function of the brain. For every rational truth in the real world there is an *upside-down* "truth" in the world of the double-bind.

This is a **Double-Bind**:

> **If you *do* have *faith* and relinquish your brain, you cannot, in reality, reach a confirmation of a truth. *The means have been taken away.***

> **If you *don't* have *faith*, and rely on your brain, you will *not* find the confirmation of the "truth" of something that is false.**

In both cases, you will be judged "guilty" of not receiving the "burning in the bosom." Again, Mormonism juxtaposes opposites, pits them against each other, and then, subtly uses the opposite (reason) for the proof of *faith* ... *which is doomed to fail.*

The Binder *divides*, pitting faith and reason against each other, and by that means, conquers. Reason *has* to be the enemy of *faith,* which in the Double-Bind is *necessary*, but not to be seen ... it becomes the *Satan* that is there, yet ... is not there. The Mormon Apostle, Boyd K. Packer said in effect that objective *reasoning might be the enemy of God.* He states, "In an effort to be objective, impartial, and scholarly a writer or a teacher may unwittingly be giving equal time to the adversary." ... "In the Church we are not neutral. We are one-sided. There is a war going on and we are engaged in it. It is a war between good and evil, and we are belligerents defending the good." (From his talk: *The Mantle Is Far, Far Greater Than The Intellect.*)

(The word "mantle" = a cloak, something that <u>covers</u>, in this case, rational truth.)

The *Closed System* is "one-sided" (only non-brain *faith* is allowed). On the one hand, it turns its back on reason, the *Open System*; on the other hand, it claims "reason" in "lip service." The dual personality in Mormonism is the "*Yes*," reason, "*But*," at the same time, it is "non-reason."

This is why members "fail" to receive the "gift" of confirmation: they are *sincere*! They are relying on their own *true* perceptions, the means to reason and Self-control, which is a brain related activity. The reason more "work" is demanded of individuals who "fail" is that their minds have not yet been "converted" to the upside-down world of programmed "Yes, but" thinking and the feelings that are attached to that view. When this is not seen, the means of survival in the real world are gradually eroded making us totally dependent and compliant to a fabricated idea that is designed, step by step, to dehumanize those who are enticed into it unknowingly.

It will be helpful to know that each step, or stage, is connected by a "hook"; the transitions between each are very subtle. In this case, the "hook" is the "but." In each stage, once the "hook" is accepted, it becomes the connecting link to the next one. This is the insidious nature of The Pattern.

Stage 4 Reversal – Double-Bind

The Double-Bind as Experienced by Women – Stage 4

Guilt – Reversal

(A very common Double-Bind is the coercion of bearing of testimonies.)

"The last straw was drawn when they expected me to offer my testimony. The missionaries had taught me that a person should create their own prayers, as opposed to repeating prayers as the Catholics do. ... That Sunday, however, after a few members had recited their chorus line (*using the same set of words*), it appeared everybody's eyes were on me. I did not get up. Immediately following the closing prayer, the missionary came to shake my hand and said, very loudly, 'we need our friend here to give her testimony.'"   Post #16 *See: Stage 1, Stages 2 – 3, #16*

Her Double-Bind:

If she *did* bear her testimony, she would be labeled *"good."*

(She would, however, in reality, be guilty of going against herself.") Guilty.

If she *didn't* bear her testimony, she would be labeled *"bad."*

(She would be going against the church and her "voluntary" commitment that must be confirmed over and over again.) "Guilty."

The Double-Bind is always FOR the BINDER, and AGAINST the BOUND, the individual Self. It is reinforced through repetition until there is no longer a Self to go against; the mind then is silenced into obedience and is labeled "good."

*   *

Double-Bind – Guilt/Fear

"After baptism I continued to ask questions ... *(Being an orphan)*, I asked them *(the missionaries)* about illegitimate orphans. They said that orphans were less valiant in the pre-existence. They were not born into homes where they would have parents and it was because of how they lived in the pre-existence. I felt sick to my stomach. I knew that if I had been taught that belief before baptism I would never have joined the church. Now that I was a member I figured that if I became the very best Mormon I could be I would win God's favor and He would forgive me for being less valiant in the pre-existence. I hoped I could clean the slate for I never wanted to come face to face with God and feel His disappointment because I had been less valiant in the pre-existence. I was always afraid to ask if God had forgiven me for what I had done in the pre-existence and how I could ask for forgiveness when I didn't know what it was I did. Or, was I suppose to be asking for forgiveness for not being valiant but valiant in what? How could I know? So I just kept trying to be a good Mormon."   Post #37 *See: Stages 1, 2 – 3, #37*

Her Double-Bind – Guilt/Fear:

She would be damned if she *did* remain a Mormon.

(It would be against herself, her own perceptions.) Guilty.

She would be damned if she *didn't* remain a Mormon.

(She would (1) not be "valiant" in this life; (2) she would forfeit her chance to work out her "repentance" for not being "valiant" in the pre-existence, plus, (3) she would then be denied entrance into the Celestial Kingdom in the next life.) "Guilty."

She would have failed in her past life, her present life and therefore, her future life: "Guilty, Guilty, Guilty."

*   *

Double-Bind – Guilt

"Right after we were married, our stake president wanted to discuss sex with us. He told us that rather than continue the old approach of inquiring into every prurient thought, the church would leave it to our discretion what sexual practices were permissible. ...This ...coming from an old guy we hardly knew who had but weeks before been asking my husband about masturbation. It was also too little, too late, for resurrecting the idea that sex between married people is okay. Being told to be fruitful and multiply is one thing, but after years of being told that sex is forbidden, evil, unclean, and transforms the woman into some revolting thing like 'used gum' or a 'half-eaten cookie,' it is unrealistic to think that normal sexual functioning could result from such constant negative conditioning."   Post #43 *See: Stage 1, #43*

The Double-Bind:

You are damned if you *do* have sex.

(Sex is forbidden, evil, and unclean; the woman is like a gardenia, once it has been touched it turns brown, and can never return to its white purity.) "Evil."

You are damned if you *don't* have sex.

(You are commanded to have sex ... to have as many children as you can; this is "Good." At the same time you are "Evil," because you break the first forbidden sex-commandment.)

*   *

Rape of the Mind, Emotions and Body – Double-Binds – Guilt and Fear

(The following is the cruelest use of the Double-Bind of all these posts ... not with an adult, but with a totally defenseless child.)

"My father was in jail for domestic abuse against my mother. My mother turned to the church for financial help because she was trying to raise me, my sister, and my brother on her own. She did have a job at a nursing home, but it wasn't enough to cover food. The Bishop agreed to help her, providing that she would clean the church. Just a few light duties: washing the windows and vacuuming, mostly. I was in charge of vacuuming. My mom had a key to the church and I would go over there when she was at work and make sure that it was all vacuumed every Saturday so that it would be ready for Sunday. (*She was only 7 years old.*) My experience all started when I ran into a counselor in the bishopric. On that particular day, I remember being very upset because I was constantly being teased by the other kids because my dad was in jail. The counselor sat me down on his lap in the chapel and asked me to tell him why I was crying. He was so kind! So wonderful! This was a man of God wanting to know about ME! I told him everything. I trusted him and was really happy for the attention! I went home that day very happy and grateful for my new friend."

(Gradually, each Saturday, this counselor began subtly to molest her. She was confused, but really didn't understand or question it...)

... "because, after all – he was a member of the bishopric. I was extremely uncomfortable with this behavior, but he always told me that I was 'special.' And that he loved me like I was his own little girl. I should never tell, because that would break the promises we had made to each other in the church. ... Once I told my mom that I didn't want to clean the church anymore, she told me that if I didn't then I would be responsible for the church taking food away from our family. Did I really want to do that? NO. I couldn't handle it."

(The molestation increased until eventually there were more than three penetrations by this counselor.)

"I just kept thinking it MUST be okay because come Sunday, he would be sitting up there on the stand and wink at me once in awhile, or lead the opening remarks and after all, this was a man called of God. If God thought that it was okay, then it must be okay." ...   Post #61

(After her baptism and in the chapel for her confirmation, this counselor stood nearby with his eyes closed, and his head bowed. She was very disturbed. The next Saturday, she tried to resist him and he roughly forced her. Fortunately, her family moved shortly after that.)

This 7 year-old child had not only to contend with one Double-Bind, but two.

Double-Bind #1.

If she *did* tell anyone: *(The counselor had told her that she would be breaking the promise that they had made in God's church.)*

If she *didn't* tell anyone: *(He would be free to continue his molestation of her.)*

Double-Bind #2.

>   If she *didn't* go to the church every Saturday to
> **vacuum:** *(Her family wouldn't have enough food to eat.)*
>
>   If she *did* go to the church: *(She would be subject to
> more abuse from the counselor.)*

*   *

The Double-Bind every member encounters in the Temple is:

>   **You will be damned if you *do* speak of the "sacred"
> oaths and penalties ...** *(made without prior knowledge)* ...
> **outside the temple.**
>
>   (You go against your "voluntary" oath and against the
> Binder.)
>
>   **You are damned if you *don't* speak of them.**
>
>   (You go against yourself; you are silenced through fear
> of bloody punishment and "Guilt.")

"I didn't say anything to anyone because you're not supposed to
discuss those things outside the temple, and I felt strange bringing
up the question in the celestial room. That was not the time to
question anyone. ... I was never prepared for that *(the penalties)*,
but my mom and dad were there, so I thought they understood
everything and it was something they did all the time."   Post #33
See: Stage 1, #33

*   *

Double-Bind – Guilt/Fear

>   (Another way to express the Double-Bind in Mormonism,
> is described by this Post.)

"Their (Mormonism) treatment of homosexuals seeking help is
appalling. While I am not gay, I was involved with a gay member
of the church, and the hell he was put through – even as he

begged for help – was appalling. Instead of self-acceptance for EVERY member, the church teaches conditional love:

> **"If you *do* this and this and this, the church/God will love you and find you worthy."**
>
> (If it is in the interest of the Binder, it will be against the self, the individual ... then, it is "good.")
>
> **"If you *do not* do this and this, you are damned for all time – starting here and starting now."**   Post #69
> *See: Stages 2 – 3, #69*
>
> (If it is for your Self, or an individual, it is against the Binder; you are then, "evil.")

Note: The Mormon Apostle, Boyd K. Packer, in his Talk to the All-Church Coordinating Council *said that all must* "set aside personal interests and all face the same way." ... *towards the organization (the Closed System), not towards the individual. He refers to individuals* "who are hurting" *as* "exceptions" *that take the church away from* "the rank and file who are trying to do what they are supposed to do and feel neglected as we concentrate on solving the problems of the exceptions." ... *In other words, the rank and file are in more need than the few individual exceptions. The church's plan for the membership is* "simplification and reduction." *In Packer's words,* "Simplification and reduction must come. Simplification and reduction will come." *This means for the general welfare of all, not for individuals. In The Pattern all individuals become an* "other" *and are reduced to the lowest common denominator; individuals not keeping up with the herd are expendable. In another culture, they would be called* "pariahs" ... outcasts. *In Mormonism, no one leaves the* "ninety and nine to save the one." (Luke 15:4) *Mormonism claims Christianity,* "Yes," "But" ... *it is teaching and living Old Testament Tribal Law. (See Part I,* One Goal, *pp. 24, 25.)*

The reason for this attitude is that Mormonism causes the problems which it claims *to hate. Mormonism needs enemies to fight as a* cloak *to hide the roots of the* cause. *They cause, deny, and then project their own guilt onto* "individuals" *who become* "strangers" *to their Tribal Laws.*

The Double-Bind as Experienced by Men – Stage 4

Double-Bind – Fear

"I've removed my web page. I've chosen an alias because I'm still trying to find a way to bring my page back. *(He had left the church and was stating his opinion on his web site.)* It was my mistake for using my real name. I felt that to do otherwise would be cowardly. I guess the joke's on me. ... the members *(of the church)* in my parents area started to mobilize. My parents were harassed by people they've gone to church with for over 20 years. Instead of exhibiting Christian-type values such as comforting them for the loss of a son from Mormonism, they received emotional blackmail instead. My father's health started to suffer as a result of it."
Post #2   *See: Stages 2 – 3, #2*

His Double-Bind:

> **If he *did* use his real name, his family (who were still members of the church) would be harassed to the point of injury.**

> **If he *didn't* use his real name, he would be false to himself by concealing his identity.**

*   *

Double-Bind – Fear/Guilt

"My earliest memories of the church, while not necessarily negative, are not really positive either. They are sort of bland; null, if you will. What I do remember are impressions of not seeing what everyone else seemed to be seeing, and feeling left out as a result. I would sit through the meetings, wondering if there was something wrong with me because I couldn't get up in front of the whole congregation and spout the same platitudes that my peers did. What prevented me from thinking and speaking as the others around me?

"My father always called me 'Mister Blunt' because I was unfailingly honest in my appraisals of people and situations. This got me into trouble more than once over the years. But, in this context, I could not testify to something which I did not really feel.

"The years passed, ... The same lack of feeling was present at my ordination, and so on through my teen years. ... I did the things what I was told to do, for to disobey my dad would bring swift retribution. I was always the 'dutiful son.' I just figured that I didn't feel anything because I wasn't 'worthy' for some strange reason or other." Post #19 *See Stages 2 – 3, #19*

The 13th Article of Faith in Mormonism says; "We believe in being honest, true ..." However,

The Double-Bind:

This young man was damned if he *was* honest.

(His honest appraisals were construed to be false; he was "bad" if he told the truth.)

He was damned if he *wasn't* honest;

(He would be going against his own integrity and would be "good" only if he lied.)

Note: Because Mormonism is a Closed System, "one-sided," there can only be one view, that of the Binder, which leaves out reason, choice and universal principles. Lip service only is given to the words "honest" and "true," as if they were being applied in the universal, rational sense. New converts are attracted by the label "truth" *and "universal principles" ... the* "Yes, we believe in being honest, true ... " *Later, the "meat," that is, the church's* true *definitions replace the universal. The universal principle of being true has to do with the individual being true to himself and with his fellowman. In Mormonism, the Church replaces the individual's identity, converting the possession of "truth" to the Church, that is, the individual disappears into the Body Politic of the Church which contains all "truth." The thinking has already been done for all its members. To go against that thinking, a member would become an individual "liar."*

*   *

Double-Bind – Guilt/Fear

"Charles, a teenager, ... mentally retarded ... who clearly didn't know right from wrong ... had been baptized ... his family were not Mormons. I didn't understand how he could have made a rational decision to be baptized into the Mormon Church, but there he was – an Aaronic priesthood holder. One day Charles told me something I will never forget. Something that really sums up Mormonism. He said that he had read some 'anti-Mormon' literature which caused a lot of doubts to enter his mind. He then visited and sought counsel with the bishop. Surprisingly, the bishop did not tell Charles to stop reading 'anti-Mormon' material. Instead he told Charles to read 15 minutes of 'anti-Mormon' material, and then read 15 minutes of the Book of Mormon or other church approved material. After having read both Charles was to determine which of *the two made him 'feel' good.*

> **"Since the 'anti-Mormon' material would obviously cause doubt and bad feelings, it was false.**
>
> (This would be against the Bound.)
>
> **"Since the 'pro-Mormon' material would make C*harles feel good, it was true.*
>
> (This was for the Binder.*)*

"This was an exercise in 'truth detection' as given by our bishop ... discern truth with your feelings, not your mind." Post #28 *See: Stages 1, 2 – 3, #28*

> *The means by which this Double-Bind could be seen, or by which a <u>rational choice</u> could be made, was not there for Charles, nor is it there for any member who cannot or does not use reason.*

*   *

Double-Bind – Guilt/Fear

(The following is the Double-Bind experienced by members when they consider leaving the church. Most have members of their family who are still active participants in Mormonism and have all been staunch members from birth.)

"I will probably receive harsh criticism from your other readers for not 'being true to myself and others,' explaining to those I love my current beliefs.   However, it's just not that easy when almost everyone I know ... is and has been a faithful LDS member and proponent their entire life ."   Post #34

The Double-Bind:

To stay in Mormonism, aids the Binder, and is against your Self ... and your family.

To leave Mormonism, divorces you from your family, and you become an "outcast."

*   *

Double-Bind #1 – Guilt/Fear

"About seven years ago, there was a PBS documentary done on the LDS Church and its missionaries.   Several returned missionaries admitted that they did not 'know' the church was true, even while they had said they did as a missionary. ... one of the LDS secrets is that there is a great deal of peer pressure on missionaries to say 'I know,' whether or not they do. I would note that while I lied, I did so while feeling caught by my obligation to serve God. I had been taught that it was my duty to serve God as a missionary, that 'every worthy young man should serve a mission.' I had been taught that those who prayed sincerely and in righteousness would receive a testimony and if they had not, one chief reason would be that they were not recognizing the answer God was giving."

If you lie, you are "good."

(You go against yourself.)

If you tell the truth, you are "bad."

(You go against the Binder.)

Double-Bind #2 "Mental Illness" – "Delusions of Grandeur"

"Further, some suggest that I was emotionally ill. There is no doubt that I was. The only question is what was the cause and the exact nature of my 'mental illness.' They suggest that, in a mild form, I was suffering from delusions of grandeur, caused by my close association with that other fellow, Brad Thompson, who happened to be my EQ president when I first came to BYU. He also, in his own way, suffered delusions of grandeur. In a way, this suggestion is no doubt true. The only question is as to whether Mormonism itself feeds such delusions."   Post #38 *See: Stages 2 – 3, #38*

> (This is another version of the promise that you "will receive" ... (fill in any blessings "given" you) ... then when it isn't fulfilled you are accused of wanting to be "the center of the Universe.")

Double-Bind:

> **If he *didn't* have faith that his blessings would be fulfilled, he would be *faithless* and "guilty."**

> **If he *did* believe they would be fulfilled, but they were not, then he was guilty of *"suffering delusions of grandeur"* in thinking that *he could expect what others had not yet received***

(*Others must be served first; each in the queue must step back ... no one can be "first."*)

*   *

Double-Bind – Guilt

"Free Agency as taught by the church: 'I am free to choose good or evil.' In practice, Mormon free agency is a sort of bondage. It amounts to:

"If I obey authority and do not think for myself then I have 'chosen' Good."

"If I do not obey authority and think for myself then I have chosen Evil."   Post #,70

Stage 5: Denial – Dehumanized

Humiliation – "Zig"

The hook of the "But" in Stage 3 led into the Double-Bind in Stage 4. The "hook" in Stage 4 was "Guilt"; whichever choice was made, the Bound was "Guilty" either against the Binder or against the Self. However, the Bound was praised as "Good" if he or she "chose" to obey the Binder and to silence the Self. Not seeing that both were negative choices, the "choice" to obey the "Good-Binder" made the reversal from Self-determination to authoritarian control complete.

The Bound has now "chosen" to be "good," which becomes the "hook" in Stage 5, and receives "Praise" from the Binder for being obedient. A true "conversion" has taken place; all "guilt" of the Self has been "washed" away; a new life with no history begins. All that is needed to keep being "Good" is to obey the Binder in all things and to reflect his mind.

The humanity and reason that existed in the Open System are now *denied* and declared the "enemy" of the Closed System of the Binder. From having one personal name, each person now shares one classificatory name with many others (*given in the Temple Ceremony*); the individual has disappeared. Obedience to *new*, secret laws is required, with punishments attached for revealing the accompanied "sacred" ordinances, the *new* name, and the penalties associated with their secret Covenants. Those who belong to this "*New* World Order" are few in number and considered part of the vanguard of this *new* Elite church. They have a Leader who oversees these *new* Covenants and this leader is also the *Guardian* over His flock of *new* converts. They are told, *He will not lead astray those who follow him.* He holds the "Keys" to the mystery of His Powers, *the mysterious Pattern of The Double-Bind*, which only He has been selected to understand and from which He can "*prophesy*." He has His Praetorian Guards to shield these Keys of the "Incomprehensible" from the general membership. They are not ready for this *"Advanced History" (which is concealed in its past secular history)*. It can only be understood under the "Mantle of the Spirit." The new converts become as "little children" who must first have *milk* before *meat;* therefore, Faith needs to take the place of Knowledge ... of The "Keys" ... the *meat.*

His Guards must fight the enemies of the "Incomprehensible," and since the Power lies in the "Keys," they must be kept hidden; *they are not secret*, they say ... however, they are too *"sacred"* for speech (= *"No, but, Yes")*. To protect these "sacred" mysteries, another "Key" is provided to keep silence imposed on His members ... the "Yes, but no, yet is" ... which says, "Yes," there may have been (a history), "but" it is no longer ... "yet" it is ... in an *advanced* way."

This is the stage of obfuscation, denial, silence and obedience. It is done "kindly" and with subtlety; the voice of the "Guardian" speaks. The members of this *New* World Order are to see it as a new *restored* "Paradise." Now being part of this Elite by association, they are all occupants of an isolated island "Paradise." All within this "Paradise" reflect this new image in every way. They each become an "Adam" or an "Eve" who are as innocent as little children. They are admonished to stay in this "pure" state and to be totally guided by their Guardian Leader.

Stage 5 and 6 is a *Zig-Zag* Double-Bind

"Milk" vs. "Meat"

Praise if you go against yourself, and guilt if you go against the Binder.

Stage 5 is the *"Zig"* part of the *"Zig-Zag"* course of two stages, *"Zag"* being that of Stage 6. The Guardian belongs to stage 5 ... the "benevolent" aspect of his dual personality; you could say he is a "Dr. Jekyll," the healer of the injuries incurred

during the Double-Bind chaos of Stage 4. In stage 6, he becomes the formerly hidden "Mr. Hyde," the opposite aspect of "Dr. Jekyll." What "Dr. Jekyll" *says* is not what "Mr. Hyde" *does*. These two stages work alternately, creating a "double-faced" character; the two acting as one; this *result* is called hypocrisy in the Real World and the basis of the Double Standard. This dual personality is also shown in Stage 3 as the "Yes" and the "But" aspects, as well as in stage 4 of the Double-Bind as the "Good" and the "Evil" aspects.

The Double Standard is caused by the Binder's theft of the good qualities of the Bound and the projection of the Binder's bad qualities onto the Bound. When *he* does anything, it is "Good." When the Bound does *the same thing*, it is "Bad." The Binder must always be "intelligent"; the Bound must always be "stupid." If there is a "Law" in the New World Order that *the Bound obeys,* then in order that the Binder may keep her (or him) in her assigned place, she is accused of being "mindless" ... that she *needs* "rules" to follow ... that is, she is condemned for not being able to think for herself. On the other hand, if *the Binder doesn't* obey the "Law," he is the "Mind" that is *above* the "Law"; he doesn't *need* the rules. The Bound is left with the implicit demand to intuit the "intelligent," *higher* Mind of the Binder ... as to when she should ... (*"Yes,"*) obey rules ... or when she should already *know* when rules are (*"But, No ..."*) *not* necessary.

This is also another double-bind. When she follows the rules, as above, she is "guilty." When she doesn't follow the rules, she is also "guilty." She walks on "egg shells" looking for a *sign* that would indicate *in advance* the Binder's illusive whim.

Even though *in years* members of the Mormon church may be considered *adults, in the growth toward maturity of mind* they are kept as *little children*, totally dependent on a Doctor *Jekyll-Shepherd* to *heal* them of their chronic child-like inability to *get things "right."* Mormonism *causes* the *evils* that it condemns and promises to heal.

The "Yes, but no, yet is."

"Yes" (reason, fact), *"But No"* (no reason or fact),

"Yet Is" (is/is not a fact)

The dual personality of the Binder is a Janus; one face looks back to the Open System (reason, which it *claims*); the other looks forward to the Closed System (no reason), then, as One entity, claims both.

Denial – Humiliation – Obfuscation
Blank-out/No-mind Dehumanization

All Real World Meanings Have Been Reversed
Into a New World Order

Experiences by Women – Stage 5

Denial

"It is extremely difficult to leave the Mormon Church. ... They will encourage you to ignore your doubts and to push them to the back of your mind, in order to keep your testimony. ... It saddens me to see LDS people walking through life with their eyes tightly closed so they won't lose their faith."   Post #5

> *Members are encouraged continually to deny reality; they reflect the Binder's denial. They are to have One Mind only ... the Mind of the Binder.*

*   *

Denial – Blank-out / No-mind – Intimidation

"When I went into the Bishop's office, I told him the reasons that I wished to be taken off the records of the church. I told him of what I had learned in the past year. He told me that he didn't want to excommunicate me because if I decided to come back it would be a long hard process – so he wanted to place me on inactive status instead. I told him that I never wanted to come back, and I wasn't going to change my mind. He said that he wanted to give me a book that was written by a General Authority, and he wanted me to read it and pray about it. I refused his offer and asked him if someone gave him a satanic bible and asked him to pray about it – if he would. He said that he wouldn't because he knew that it was wrong, and I told him he had just proven my point. Also in the meeting, he asked me if I had any questions, so I asked him about the holes that I found in the doctrine of the Mormon Church. He didn't really answer any of my questions, but just beat around the bush, and ended with his testimony that he knew the Mormon church was true without a shadow of a doubt. He told me that he wouldn't be able to grant my request to have my records removed until he had talked to the Stake President. It's been over a year now, and this process still hasn't been completed." Post #6

("Yes," do question ... "But," no answers ... "Yet," he "knows" without a shadow of a doubt.)

The bishop denied his own reasoning powers; plus, in refusing to acknowledge her request, he was denying her right to reason and choose for herself, and, as an extension of that mind-set, he employed silence and delaying tactics ... as if the meeting had never taken place. Blank-out.

* *

Denial of the Old, plus a New Identity

"The church offered me a sense of identity. I received endless praise and encouragement when I continued to eagerly learn, absorbing information like a sponge. The sense of elitism (WE had the TRUTH that no one else had) made me feel special. For a while, the church fulfilled a strong need. I finally fit in." Post #13
See: Stage 1, #13

* *

Denial – "Guardian"

"I was absent from church on Sunday for 2 weeks, a few members called me saying they were 'concerned.' That is actually a code word. They were simply coercing me into coming to church. I was naive enough to think they were worried about my health and reassured them I was in good health. On the third Sunday, I was out of town. They called and left messages on my answering machine. I came back home very late and did not return any calls. The next day, three officials from the church came to my place of work, but visitors must state the reason for their visit and personal visitors are not allowed at my work place. By that evening, they had called one of my bosses because 'they were concerned.' I was furious ..."   Post # I6 *See: Stages 1, 2 – 3,4, #16*

> *Her reasonable answer that she was in good health was not accepted nor acknowledged. The identity of the Binder as the "concerned Guardian," was a subtle coercing ... she was not being "obedient" in her attendance at church. Numbers and records are an obsession in Mormonism. Members of the church are chastised if their assigned "contacts" don't attend regularly.*

*   *   *

Denial – Dehumanization – Elitism

"I was taught that I was 'better than the rest,' 'a superior being in the preexistence,' 'I would become a great goddess and populate universes.' That was the exterior of my family."   Post #20

> *What is not taken into account when a human being begins to assume the "mantle" of a "god" or a "goddess," is that they begin to deny their identity as human beings and consequently all the associated characteristics that go with being human. They become dehumanized and placed on pedestals, which is a* demotion *not an elevation.*

*   *   *

Denial – "Guardian" – Silence

"I was afraid to read them (*books by ex-Mormons)* and thought that I would probably feel a dark evil presence while I read them and I was sure that by the actions I'd already taken (*having read other non-Mormon literature),* that Satan was really trying to get at me. ... I didn't have that feeling at all. Finally, after years, probably since around the time I was baptized, I felt a sense of peace wash over me! I really felt free and life was starting to make some sense to me. It was like this horrible dark cloud that had hovered over my head was lifted.

"I had thought all the inconsistencies I had found over the years were from lack of knowledge about the church (well, I was right, in a way). The times I had asked questions to bishops, they were brushed aside. I was told, 'You worry about things too much that shouldn't bother you,' or 'You don't need to think about those things.' I was never given answers. It was a relief to finally be able to piece things together, and I finally felt a lot less ignorant.

"It's been a struggle with family ... I told my mom one night, I rambled on for 20 minutes, then she said, 'Before you go any further, let me tell you that I think the same way.' I was happy to hear that and that she had not found the things in the temple to be quite right either. I've always had a scary feeling in those places. But now she doesn't want to discuss it whenever I bring it up because it depresses her. The other day, she asked me if I'd read a rebuttal book her Home Teachers told her about and I started explaining why it wasn't true, and she said, 'I knew I shouldn't have brought it up.' She doesn't want to lose the close ties she has with her mom and sister." Post #29

*   *

Denial – No-mind – Obfuscation

"My most painful Mormon experience was learning that having faith in something does not necessarily make it true. ... There was something reckless and impulsive about telling a dying woman that she would be healed simply because my sister got a feeling that it was true. ... I have heard of or been witness to many other instances when blessings that promised healing or Patriarchal Blessings have turned out wrong. My great uncle's Patriarchal Blessing said that he would live to see the second coming of Christ. He died about 30 years ago at the age of 73. (An uninspired Patriarch?)

"I wondered too. The old there-are-some-things-the-Lord-doesn't-mean-for-us-to-understand explanation would not salve over my doubting that time. One thing that I have found over and over in Mormonism is that an explanation or excuse can be divined for just about ANYTHING that doesn't sit quite right. And if something can't be explained away, members are told to rely on faith. 'If we could explain everything then there would be no faith and without faith we couldn't be tested.' Yes, I've heard it all." Post #30

*   *

Elitism

"'So and so isn't a member, but she is a really nice person' Putting qualifications on people via member or not."

Zig-Zag

"Hypocrisy with the capital H there! I knew many Mormons and Elders who spoke and taught one thing, then turned around and did the other. This was one of the main things that really turned my stomach."   Post #32 – 2 *See: Stage 1, #32 – 2*

*   *

"Yes ... No ... Yet is." – Humiliation

"I knew that I was going on a mission for the right reason. I only wanted to share the True Gospel and was filled with the Book of Mormon stories of faithful missionaries converting thousands. France was known as a difficult mission, but that only strengthened my desire to be a mighty missionary, filled with faith, finding all those special spirits just waiting for us to have enough faith to find them and convert them to Mormonism.

"Imagine my dismay when instead, I arrived in France to be told that my obedience was more valued than my faith ... the people of Bordeaux were NOT INTERESTED in our message. I wept every morning and night, and entered into a depression which lasted my entire mission, with varying degrees of severity. I called President Wheelwright and told him I needed to go home (this after 2 weeks in the field!) He convinced me to wait until our visiting General Authority (Brother Hale) came to inspire us with his guidance. My most vivid memory (backed up by my extensive journal entries) of Brother Hale's talk was that he berated us for being poor missionaries. The whole reason we could not convert people was due to our pitiful lack of faith. He berated the elders by insinuating that the sisters were far more faithful than they were (evidently to be compared poorly to a woman was his idea of the ultimate humiliation). I felt like crawling under my chair, for I knew that we could not be any better than the elders, for we were too pitiful, too."
Post #42

"Yes," faith is the most important thing for a missionary.

"No." Obedience is the priority.

"Yet," faith *is* the most important ... you fail because you don't have enough faith.

She was humiliated at the insinuation that the elders were even below their sisters in their abilities to have Faith. This was also a double-bind.

*   *

"What was, is not, yet is" – Silence – Projection

"I feel that the Church leadership is not inspired. It would be laughable, if not so pathetic, that *(Apostle)* Packer could actually say that the three greatest threats to the church are homosexuals, feminists, and so-called intellectuals. ... Neither could I stomach the recent purge that forced out several intellectuals like Paul Toscano and D. Michael Quinn. This is particularly troubling in light of the iron grip the church keeps on its own history, preventing free inquiry into its origins, as if it had something to fear. In the end, the two statements that 'The glory of God is intelligence,' and 'When the Brethren speak, the thinking has been done,' are simply mutually incompatible." Post #43 *See: Stage 1,4, #43*

"What was, is not, yet is:"

The Mormon history *that was* ...

is not the true history,

yet is ... the "advanced history."

Zig-Zag **Double-Bind:**

Zig: **What is said:** "The glory of God is intelligence."

Zag: **What is done:** "The thinking has been done, when the Brethren speak."

To have "intelligence" in the Mormon church is to repeat verbatim what you have been told you are supposed to "know." This begins in childhood by statements like this: "All I need to know is what I learned in Primary." In other words, "milk" ... forever.

*   *

Obedience – Perfection

"I was always shocked when I was called to a position and wondered if the Bishop really received a message from God to call me to that position since I knew I wasn't worthy. But in talking to other women I found out I wasn't alone but was always told that God calls us to positions for our personal growth and that by accepting these callings we would be on the road to perfection. I accepted everything I was told as gospel truth ... "   Post #53
See: Stages 1, 2 – 3, #53

> *The guilt from Stages 3 and 4 carry over and is added to this stage; one never feels entirely "worthy." Perfection, aiming for god or goddess status and the Celestial Kingdom, is another "carrot on the end of the stick." Obedience is all that is required in stage 5; **faith** has become automatic because "the thinking has already been done." Obedience, Work, and Proselytizing for the "up-building of the Kingdom here on earth" become one's whole life, the "road to perfection" ... of perfect obedience.*

*   *

Obedience – Silence

"As I got older, there were more and more things I found that I disagreed with. I thought something must be wrong with me, because here are all of these adults telling me that the church is true and that they knew it was true. When I would ask questions about something said, I was told not to question the leaders of the church. If I didn't agree with something someone said, I was told that I just had to accept that it was from God and that it was His word. We were to never question or disagree with the leaders of the church."   Post #55

*   *

"Was, is not, yet is."

"I do not believe in polygamy, which the church teaches will be a part of the eternal plan in Heaven. (In the 80's, seminary lessons included this fact, now, as the church is ever-changing, they claim that information about this hasn't been 'revealed' yet. This is from missionaries that I spoke with shortly before I left the church.)" Post #55

> *Polygamy "**Was**," before it was outlawed by the U. S. Government; "**Is not**," because it hasn't been "revealed" yet; "**Yet is**" ... plural marriages are still being performed in the temple for the next life.   (This is another version of "advanced history," that is, that "**Will be**.")*

*   *

"Was, is not, yet is." – Silence as an Answer

> *(This is the next stage in the experience of the 7 year old girl who had been molested and raped by a Bishop's counselor in the church building.   As an adult the psychological and emotional unearned guilt she carried from these traumas was devastating.)*

"... I came across the book 'Miracle of Forgiveness': by Spencer W. Kimball. He had been my favorite prophet, and I was always in awe of him.   But his statement regarding chastity left me feeling like I had been kicked in the stomach:

'Restitution for Loss of Chastity'

Also far-reaching is the effect of chastity.   Once given or taken or stolen it can never be regained.   Even in a forced contact such as rape or incest, the injured one is greatly outraged.   If she has not cooperated and contributed to the foul deed, she is of course in a more favorable position.   There is no condemnation where there is no voluntary participation.   It is better to die in defending one's virtue than to live having lost it without a struggle.

"All of the past came rushing back to me with such a force that I was in bed for days. ... I made an appointment with my Bishop.   I told him of the abuse that my uncles did to me. *(After the molestation by the counselor, she had been sexually abused when she was about 9 years old by her father's brothers ... the father that had been jailed for abusing his wife.)* (I didn't make any mention of my questions regarding church discrepancies at this time.) He said all the right words, 'It's okay, You are forgiven ... It isn't your fault, etc. ...' Then I showed him what I had read in 'The Miracle of Forgiveness.' He told me that the book was 'outdated' for today and that those words wouldn't stand in my situation. I was again confused. The prophet of the Lord wrote this book, and it wouldn't stand? It was outdated? But, I did find comfort in the fact that this Bishop said he would do anything he could to help me rid myself of my past so that I could go on with my life. He and I had a few more sessions until I felt better about things. He did everything he could to help me and I began to rely on his talks with me a great deal. I felt good about my life.

"But the anxiety and panic whenever I would go to church would continue. I thought it must be God's way of telling me I didn't belong. The Bishop would insist that perhaps I wasn't 'doing my part' by reading the Book of Mormon. That I should study it more diligently. God would give me comfort if I TRULY seeked it. ... I finally told the Bishop about my experience with the counselor in the Bishopric between the ages of 7 and 8. *(Before and after baptism.)* He immediately got a cold look on his face and shut off completely. He told me right then that he was unable to help me any further and that he wouldn't be able to speak to me again until I got professional help. I would try and call him at home and he refused my calls. (My calls were always a priority before.) I felt abandoned again. I felt alone and discarded and violated. I had shared things with this Bishop that I hadn't shared with anyone and he just plain didn't care anymore. I was suicidal. I didn't believe that God could or would love me if His Bishop couldn't love and accept me. I truly believed that with all of my heart." Post #61 *See: Stage 4, #61*

> **"Yes,"** " *it is better to die in defending one's virtue than to live having lost it without a struggle."*
>
> *(... even if you were a child ... had no choice of your environment ... were caught in double-bind situations imposed by authoritarian figures representing "God" that you had been trained to obey and trust ... who proceeded to rape your mind and your body? How could she have mentally or physically defended herself?)*

"But, no," *"The Miracle of Forgiveness" book is "outdated" for today."*

(Even though it was written by a prophet "who will never lead you astray.")

"Yet, is" *not outdated.*

*(This was implied when the bishop cut her off completely and erected a wall of impenetrable silence ... abandoning her. In The Pattern, **silence, to the Bound, means unspoken assent ... an assumption of "guilt."** This, also, is the blankout of any guilt on the part of the abuser; it has been projected to the abused.)*

*   *

Silence as the Binder's Denial.

"To this day, no one has ever asked why I left the church: it's Not To Be Mentioned, by mutual silent agreement. Don't rock the spiritual boat." Post # 69 *See: Stages 2 – 3, 4, #69*

Experiences by Men – Stage 5

Denial – Revisionism, History Rewritten – New Time Obfuscation and Deceit

Omission

"President Kimball and his wife toured Finland in 1975 when I was a missionary. ... What was really striking was when Sister Kimball spoke to us. In part of her talk she digressed from an apparently memorized (from being given so many times) speech and talked about an experience at the University of Utah. She took an institute class there while her husband was an apostle and was troubled by what the instructor (an LDS liberal evidently) was presenting to the class. She expressed her troubles with her husband who lightly dismissed them. The casual dismissal was a problem for her. What is fascinating now is that she would have expressed any doubt at all to us and it was clearly out of context with the talk she was giving. This digression occurred in mid-thought on another subject. When we got our transcripts of the talk, I noticed that this was not included. Here was history being rewritten right before my eyes."

Revisionism

"LDS History: The visitation of 1820 of God and Jesus to Joseph Smith has been shown by the mass of information on the supposed event to have never occurred. The date conflicts with other recorded historical events and even with Joseph Smith's mother's account of her son's history! No one ever mentioned this revelation until Smith dictated it 18 years later! It plays no role at all in Mormon history until the 1860's. His early hand written account (1831 – 1832 diary) does not even mention God the father visiting. He forgot that God visited him? That is absurd. As Smith got older, he got bolder in his claims of power and visitations and the creating of an imaginary history is just part of that. He did this when there were fewer eyewitnesses around who could claim such events never happened or did not happen the way he testified to. When a Mormon reads the official history today it appears everything occurred in a certain order when in reality most items were back dated and created out of thin air to lend credibility to the ever increasing stories."

History Rewritten

"The official Mormon history has been heavily rewritten. This is one of the most disturbing things I discovered in our research of the church. Even the official History of the Church is only 40% Joseph Smith's writings when it is still claimed to be 100%. The 40% has been rewritten so as to be 'faith promoting' and the 60%, which was not his writing at all, was selectively chosen from other people's writings and rewritten to make him out to be something he was not."

Deceit

"I believe deceit goes on at all levels of the church by seasoned members, with much of it well intended, but done with incredible ignorance. The degree of deceit varies with the intelligence, knowledge and church position of the seasoned members involved. When a member of the church brings up a historical or doctrinal problem, a seasoned member has learned how to give pat answers which give a superficially satisfactory resolution. For example, the question of why is the temple so similar to Masonry may get asked. The standard answer is that Masonry goes back to Solomon's temple. Any reasonable inquiry into that myth will show it to be absurd historically. This does seem however to satisfy one who does not dig any deeper and does not want to be troubled. Senior members of the church dole out such dribble all the time. In many cases they do not know themselves and give such a response because it was satisfactory to them. More intelligent individuals, such as Hugh Nibley, use their prolific creation of unrelated materials to confuse the question and the normal church [member] then concludes all must be well because someone wrote so much about it and the member is too overwhelmed to be troubled anymore. Is this deceit? I think it is. A seasoned member usually wants to give the impression of having superior knowledge and spirituality with no doubts expressed verbally about his or her faith. This facade is required in leadership positions and is also required in most Mormon social circles. The senior levels of the church are composed of individuals who hide behind their positions of trust and are experts at giving great impressions. This is subtle and powerful deception." Post #1

* *

Elitism

"To be a Mormon takes a lot of dedication and time. The average service on Sunday is over three hours, and that's not counting other activities during the week. The Church makes sure its members are always involved, which is one of its selling points. Mormons are made to feel important." Post # 2 *See: Stages 2 – 3, 4, #2*

* *

What is "said." – What is done.

"I felt like I needed to atone for the sins of my parents *(The...* drank beer at family picnics, opened their grocery Sunday, and drank coffee every morning; his moth* *smoking. His closest Mormon friend taunted him.)* It seemed to me that becoming a super Mormon was the only way I could be accepted by my Mormon friends and neighbors. I was determined to be a saint. I attended church every Sunday, went through four years of seminary even though only three were required for graduation, begged my dad to close the store on Sunday, tried to get my mother to quit smoking, read the scriptures regularly, prayed about everything, and dreamed of the day I could go on a mission.

"I'd pleaded with my dad not to open the store on Sunday, but when I was 16 I went to work for the bishop in our ward. He raised fruit and sold it at a fruit stand on the highway. You guessed it. He kept the stand open on Sunday. I also realized that I'd idealized the lives of many of the neighbors. I later discovered that under the surface of several of these Sunday perfect families existed a cauldron of anger, tension, and abuse that did not exist in our home."   Post #4

*   *

Obedience – History: "What was, is not."

"I was married ... in the Seattle, Washington temple on May 3, 1984. I attended that temple with the belief that I would be instructed in sacred and ancient ceremonies, right from the Lord himself. As was expected of me, I obediently promised to slit my throat etc., rather than reveal the secrets of the temple. I was surprised to learn in 1989 from a Mormon who wanted me to 'come back to the temple, because I would like it better now' that the Lord had changed his mind yet again, and redone his sacred temple ceremony. Even as a Mormon who did not yet understand that the temple ceremony is really a Masonic ceremony copied word for word, I knew that something was wrong! Why would God just suddenly change his mind about his own 'sacred ceremony,' eliminating the 'penalties' and other sacred portions? Maybe God is rather a 'politically correct' God. When confronted with opposition on the issue of polygamy, he simply changes his stance on it. When confronted with Civil Rights he ignores his 'prophet' who said, 'If there was one drop of Negro blood' a black man could never hold the Priesthood, and caves in under the pressure. When people like me are made uncomfortable with the temple's bloody oaths, God just rewrites the program. How convenient for the leadership of the Mormon Church to have such a changeable, malleable, salable God."   Post #14

In time, with newer converts, the old history will have been forgotten by omission and will become the "advanced history" ... the "meat" that cannot be understood by the finite mind; only the revised history will now be taught and remembered, as was done with the History of Joseph Smith and is currently being done with Brigham Young. The new Mormon "history" now mentions only two wives of Brigham, the first having died before his second marriage. The original history recorded that Brigham Young had a total of 55 wives. The omission by revision is the "milk" that promotes "faith." The "meat" contains the hidden facts that "yet are, and will be."

*   *

Dehumanization

"We were told in no uncertain terms by our mission president, ... that our most important job as a missionary was to see people baptized, period. In addition, the regional representative at that time, Gene R. Cook ... told us in various meetings that our job was to BAPTIZE, and that we were not to worry about whether or not they were Truly ready – that was between them and God... They would have these big mission-wide conferences, and the leaders would get up and tell the Elders & Sisters that we should be focusing on NUMBERS." Post #19 *See: Stages 2 – 3, 4, #19*

Denial – Dual Personality – Silence

" ... if faith, as they like to say, is the knowledge of things unseen, it is also the ignorance of things known, and once the ignorance is removed, the faith is sure to follow. That is why it's so important for cult-like religions to keep their flock in the dark. On the other hand, someone who gains knowledge has a distinct advantage if he wants to play the game, even if he plays with altruistic motives, which I'm certain most do.

"For example, I had a companion in Sweden who lived a double-life without apparent strain. He was a charismatic fellow who had little trouble converting people to the church (although they usually stopped attending as soon as he was sent to another town), and he suffered no qualms about hanging out in the beer halls with the ladies after the sun had gone down. He was, last time I talked to him, a bishop. I had called him, as I was wont to do every couple of years ... the last time we talked, I made the mistake of asking him point blank, 'You don't really believe all those stories about the golden plates and the angels that took them away, do you?' There was an awkward silence, and then he said, 'America was built on freedom of religion!' The anger in his voice discouraged my probing his obtuse response, for the point here was that I'd breached the line, broken the code of silence, threatened the veil of deniability." Post #23

*   *

Denial – History Rewritten

"I was in the ward library going through one of the Church History books ... This book contained some writings from Joseph Smith's personal journal. I read, with my own eyes, from Joseph Smith's own journal that he and the church had no official opinion on the plight of the black slaves in America during this time. He wrote in his journal that he did not think the black slaves should be freed. I sat back in total disbelief. Up to that point, I was told by church members and church literature that the reason the Mormons were driven out of Missouri was because the Mormons were 'anti-slavery,' and that the 'Gentile' settlers of Missouri wanted to enter the Union as a slave state."

"Yes. No. Yes."

"I was recently amused by the behavior of current Mormon prophet Gordon B. Hinckley. He was interviewed by Time Magazine a few months ago. Time asked Hinckley about the Mormon Doctrine of men becoming gods. Hinckley answered that he didn't know much about the doctrine and that it was not being taught, but he admitted once hearing something about it. Well, that was pretty much a text book definition of a lie. A short time later at General Conference, Hinckley tells the Saints that the media 'mis-reported' him, and not to rely on the media for spiritual guidance." Post #28 *See: Stages 1, 2 – 3, 4, #28*

*   *

"No. Yes. Yes/No."

"Most of my class work at BYU dealt with either the study of computers or the study of theology – two fields that have little intersection therefore no controversy. Biology 100, however, was different. Here we were taught evolution which I knew to be in conflict with the opinions of *(Apostle)* Boyd K. Packer and Bruce R. McConkie. All four biology teachers stood in front of the 200+ students in the Joseph Smith Auditorium and declared, 'We are not here to tell you that evolution is a partial explanation of the origin of the species. We are here to say that all life forms, including humans, evolved from lower life forms. Man evolved from apes.' They went on to 'prove' their statement using the fossil record, DNA comparisons and so on. Then they quoted David O. McKay as saying, 'The LDS church has no official position on the theory of evolution.' To me, this was a stunning contradiction because many of the church leaders clearly taught that evolution was a false doctrine." Post #35

* *

"Is, Is not, Yet is." – Dual Personality

"I wrote down some thoughts about the Mormon perspective. This has helped me see why it's so difficult to leave the LDS church. These points are all official doctrines of the Church and perspectives that are regularly ingrained into the membership. What blows me away now is that maintaining just a couple of these perspectives often keeps a Mormon in the Church. *(He lists 19 official doctrines.)*

(#11) "When an Apostle or Prophet says something that is accepted to be true, he is directly inspired by God. When he says something that turns out to be false, he was speaking as a man. But either way, it's not to matter to you. These men will never lead you astray." Post #36

* *

"Does. Does Not. Yet Does."

"Heber J. Grant, who later became the Mormon leader and prophet, reigning during the depression, was earlier in life made stake president. In stake conference at the time of being made stake president, he bore his testimony, saying, 'I believe the gospel is true.' Some members of the church protested about this to one general authority. The GA replied, 'He knows the gospel is true, but he does not know that he knows it.'" Post #38 *See Stages 2 – 3, 4, #38*

*   *

Denial – Blank-out – History

"It started to get clearer to me that somehow, some way, there was a huge empire built around these fabulous claims of the early to mid 1800s that somehow mutated sociologically so that few people continued to associate the church's culture with Brigham Young and Joseph Smith, but rather with the wholesome image of today as an organization with warm, touchy feelings, and a lot of great 'programs' for its members. It is interesting to observe that when these doctrinal and historical problems surface, there are numerous homilies and alibis that are used by the Mormon faith to bully its members from crossing the line from faith to rational thought. The following two are especially convenient: 'God's ways are not Man's Ways' and 'In the last days, even the very elect will be deceived,' and they are extremely effective. At least they were for me as they succeeded in cowering me into submission for the majority of my life."   Post #44

. *   *

Obfuscation – History – Denial

"The reporter *(from the Los Angeles Times)* asked *(President)* Hinckley to comment about the 1993 Branch Davidian tragedy and about the Mormon Church's evolution from 'fringe' sect to respectability. President Hinckley – a practiced, high-viscosity media hand – made some noises about religious freedom but carefully emphasized that the Church has nothing to do with 'fringe' groups and that the 'law' can deal with them: 'We just plow our own furrow and go forward,' concluded Hinckley.

"Curious, isn't it, how Hinckley – who as a court historian for the LDS Hierarchy expended a lot of indignation over the supposed indifference to the Mormons' plight displayed by 19th century leaders – now considers such indifference to be a virtue – at least, when it's some other 'fringe group' that's on the receiving end of federal persecution.

"Like many others, Hinckley compared Waco to Jonestown. But an apter comparison is to Nauvoo: A young, charismatic, sexually omnivorous 'prophet' organizes an insular, theocratic community with its own militia. However, while we can document Joseph Smith's extracurricular sexual exploits, less is known about the reliability of the accusations against David Koresh. (Joseph's 'revelation' is in the LDS Standard Works, after all.) Furthermore, Koresh – whatever else might be said about him – displayed no such grandiose ambitions as those animating the organizer of the Council of Fifty, the commander-in-chief of the 'war department' of the Church, the Masonically-connected independent Presidential candidate, and self-crowned 'Prophet, Priest and King over Israel on Earth' – that is, Joseph Smith.

Denial

"The gentleman from message number 47 mentioned how he had a little 'box' in the back of his mind where he stored his doubts and misgivings. This phrase resonated with my own interview a little more than a week ago, when I was 'called in' by my Stake President as a result of letters I had written to the First Presidency. ... He seemed genuinely concerned about me, at least within his familiar frame of reference. But he invited me to 'find a little box where you can keep all of these concerns' while I got on with the business of being a typical Mormon; I told him that I couldn't do that any longer, and that such an effort was undermining my peace of mind and making me physically ill.

"We went the usual rounds of off-putting, temporizing tactics – the recital of lines like 'someday we'll understand when all the facts are in,' that 'we must have faith like a little child,' ad nauseam. I explained to my President that ... faith can serve as a shortcut to truth, but it cannot justify persistence in error; faith can help us learn the truth, but it cannot alter tangible facts." Post #64

*   *

History – "Yes. No. Yes."

"Apostle Bruce R. McConkie admitted that Brigham Young did teach that Adam was God, and that the church has indeed lied about its own history. He says that Brigham Young was wrong, but he has gone to the Celestial Kingdom; but if you believe what Brigham Young taught about that, you will go to hell. The fact that the church can put a 'positive spin' on these admissions is truly mind-boggling." Post #66

Stage 6: Accusation – Demonization

"Not I, but you ..." – Guilt/Shame

If Stage 5 was Praise for Obedience causing Euphoria, Stage 6 is the Accusative stage of being Dis-Obedient, causing Shame. The "hook" for Stage 5 was the label "Good"; in Stage 6 the "hook" has the label "Evil." These are the two faces of the Binder, the Guardian and the Enforcer, the "Yes" personality and the "No" ("but") personality. The effect is that we, as members of the church, become emotionally battered "children"; we can never totally be "Good" because of the "But," and we are continually "Evil" because it is "Not the Binder who is guilty; but we who are guilty." This is the Body Politic that has only One Mind; the individual mind is the enemy. Either you are Obedient and "Good" or you are Dis-Obedient and "Evil."

However, you are not allowed to be totally either! If you were totally "Good"; you couldn't be "Saved"; if you were totally "Evil," you would be an outcast and not a contributor to the "up-building of the Kingdom" of the Binder. In the latter case, however, you have a "second chance," you can repent, confess your "sins," be "forgiven" ... and "grateful." Members are, in reality, not meant to be totally "Good" nor totally "Evil," but in between ... never sure they are "Good" and worthy, and never really knowing for sure where to draw the line on "Evil"; the "Good" gets further and further away (you will never know until *the* Judgment Day whether or not you've been good "enough"), and what is termed "Evil" keeps changing according to the needs of the Binder; the chains of "Evil" get shorter and shorter in order to keep the souls of the Bound closely chained to Him. It matters not what the changes are, *as long as the Flock is "Facing One Way"* ... towards the Binder, reflecting *always* His changing Mind. This is accepted because *"His ways are not man's ways."* This is believed because "man," as an individual thinker, no longer exists. The only hope of the Bound being Judged "Good" is to reflect the Mind of the Binder in all things, knowing that The Binder's ways are mysterious and that He holds the "Keys" that unlock the Knowledge of All Things. *The thinking has already been done.*

As a result, His Magnanimous, All-Knowing image as the Guardian is reinforced, and the Flock is again reassured of His Great Goodness ... and Power.

Stage 6 is closely associated with Stage 3 in that the agreement to "aid" the Contractor in just one instance (His "Yes, But") is now claimed by Him (in Stage 6) as a contract *you* initiated in which *you* "*chose*" to do all the work by *yourself.* This is the "Not I, but *you,*" (have "chosen" and are "guilty"). It is then *your* honor that is at stake, not His. This new "hook," like the others, deepens and compounds the unearned guilt of the Bound; it also deepens the fear that the Bound person feels towards the Enforcer/Guardian. This is a "flip-flop" from the Guardian image or, as I call it, the "Zag" of "Zig-Zag." These two stages could also be called by other appellations such as, "Dr. Jekyll and Mr. Hyde:" The Double-Standard, the Dual Personality, or, as One entity, The Thief.

The Binder in this stage claims all of the good characteristics of the Bound and conversely projects onto the Bound all of His negative characteristics; more "Guilt" is applied to the Bound through this projection. The Bound is accused of not being "valiant" to "commitments," "covenants" and "oaths" made to the Binder; extreme penalties and punishments are predicted for Dis-Obedience. These are all precipitated in consequence of Stage 5.

In Stage 5, the Bound has been Obedient, worked hard, reflected the mind of the Binder, and received Praise for complete dedication. The Euphoria of being one of the Elite is there, but the neglected reality of excessive use of the human energy of the body begins to take its toll; there has been no time for the Self which needs nourishment ... it has been forgotten. The Binder does not see the Bound as being human ... the Bound must *not* be human ... to be human is *facing the other way.* However, the body and brain that is being denied can reach the breaking point; doubts arise along with complaints. They are expressed ... and the next stage of the Enforcer begins.

Projection: "Not I, but you are guilty." – *Zag*

Accusation: Projection – Guilt/Shame – Threats and Intimidation – Fear – Demonization

---

Experiences by Women – Stage 6

Zig: Obedience – Sacrifice ... of time, work, money, teaching, ... – Dehumanized

"And I was serious ... about God and religion, which of course meant the LDS church. Every piddly little baby-sitting or lawn-care chore I did and got paid for, you'd better believe I took ten percent of that out and tithed it. At age 15 I taught Sunday School to 7-year-olds. I also went on a youth temple trip (*when she lived in Detroit and the temple was in Washington DC).* I prayed daily. I attended church meetings faithfully. I fasted every fast Sunday, and gave my heartfelt testimony ... I really believed..."

Zag: Accusation – Shame – Demonized

(The prelude to this post is listed in Stage 1 and Stages 2 – 3, Post #3.)

"I met my future husband one Sunday ... We dated (chastely, might I add!) for a year. We were married in the Washington D.C. temple. I was 18, he was 23. ... My husband was an exemplary holder of the Melchizedek priesthood. He was the kind of man who would roll out of bed at 4 am on a Monday morning in January to go to the hospital and give someone a blessing, then go on to work ... Eight months after (*the birth of her son)* my husband was diagnosed with inoperable brain cancer. My husband's illness lasted about 3 and a half years altogether, and most of that time he was able to function normally in all respects. He held various positions in the ward, continued to work and pay a full tithe, etc. Late in the game when he became more disabled, he and I were treated atrociously by members of the ward. Sure, on Sunday mornings when we arrived at church, elders fell all over each other vying for the privilege of lifting his wheelchair out of the trunk, or lifting him out of the car and into it (an easy task which I needed no help with) but when it came to things which demanded just a wee bit more of them, it was a different story. ...

"For a while I had an arrangement with the RS *(Relief Society)* that one of the sisters would watch my boys (in the meantime we had found time to have another son!) for one day each week. Mind you, this was during the last year of my husband's life when he was virtually helpless and I was his sole caregiver. One day each week, a different sister would arrive at my home in the morning ... to pick up my two kids ... This lasted about four weeks. At that time, the RS president came to my house. She said, haltingly, 'I don't know how quite to say this, but ... well, the sisters are coming to your house each week to pick up your sons, and they say when they arrive that your house is pretty messy ... and then they return in the evening, it's still very untidy ... and, well, frankly, some of the sisters are wondering how wisely you're using this time ...' I could tell you how deeply I was hurt by this, but that would take forever and a day ..." Post #3 *See: Stages 1, 2 – 3, #3*

> *This kind of inhumane treatment is due to the dehumanization each member goes through in Stage 5. They lose their identities as human beings because in this* New World Order *they are to forget they once had a Self, individual emotions, or a brain that could think; they now live only for admittance into the Celestial Kingdom, and for that privilege they must obey and work incessantly. They are no longer individuals. No one is supposed to get sick or stop working; this would be a sign of a lack of Faith. This leads to the "sacrifice" of all that you humanly have or own. The Flock reflects and repeats what the Binder has said to them, and through imitation they "do unto others" ... that is, they treat (judge) others as they have been treated (judged). This means that the dual personality of the Binder is also played out by the members; what is said and what is done are two different things. In Stage 5, the Binder is the Guardian; he "says" he is the protector of widows and orphans. In Stage 6, He becomes the Accuser of the innocent and Demonizes them.*

This non-human mind-set has far reaching consequences. If I am not allowed to claim myself, not allowed to be human, then other members of the flock are not allowed to be human either. In this respect I become my "brother's keeper." That equates to "If I can't be human, you can't be human," and all that that entails. To be human, to be able to think, is to be the enemy of the Binder, and the Flock must all "face one way" ... away from those that are human. Therefore, to be human is to be "evil."

As the protector of widows and orphans He claims He is the Guardian of these unfortunate exceptions. As the Accuser, He does not recognize them; they have become human; they have human frailties; they must have sinned and therefore brought it on themselves. They are no longer contributors to His Kingdom, because of Sin. To aid these "fallen" humans would be to "pamper" them, not help them. His Judgment is that they need more "character"; in fact, they are "lazy"; they can get sympathy from others of their kind ... other "individuals." "I am not leaving them, they are leaving me!" "Not I, but they are guilty."

At first, in the case above, the humane Words (a reflection of the Binder as Guardian) were translated into token actions. The elders would give unneeded token help to their "brother" but felt no compassion to give substantial practical help. The Relief Society "sisters" also gave token help to their "sister" (one day each week for 4 weeks) as the complete fulfillment of their creed. "Yes," our creed is still the same, "But," the Binder needs us more than you do." Mock sympathy at this point turns to accusations. The wife now has a character flaw; she is now labeled "lazy" because she cannot do all the things she was able to do before she became full-time caregiver to her dying husband. The children needed care too. What she needed, as a human being, was understanding and emotional support, as well as physical help. Instead, practical help was withdrawn, and accusation replaced sympathy and understanding. Being labeled "lazy" was a form of "demonization" ... as not being on the side of the Binder. Those not for the Binder are for Satan and are "evil." She and her husband and small children were no longer able to keep up with the marching Flock ... they were expendable. To be human is to be worthless ... unworthy.

The consequence of the above is to set brother against brother, and sister against sister; men betraying men ... women betraying women. This betrayal of others is a two-edged sword. It breeds hidden anger, resentment, and even hatred towards the ones they profess to love and have denied, which is a projection of their own personal anger, resentment and hatred that they feel towards themselves at the loss they have suffered ... their own unwitting betrayal of themselves. This hardening of their hearts turns them back to face the Binder for reinforcement against themselves with even greater allegiance. Plus, the example of what happens to others when they show their humanness remains in the memory and fear becomes the incentive to follow the straight and narrow way of the Binder. The Bound then embrace even more their vanishing into the center of the Flock for "comfort"; the sick and the lame are the ones relegated to the fringes to manage for themselves their individual survival.

The tragedy is that this transition happens so subtly and fraudulently that it can't be detected while it is happening. It is usually a crisis of some kind, or a sudden tragedy, that causes the sleeping Self to wake up.

*   *

"Not I, but you ..."

"... finally, I just couldn't continue (*to*) pretend to believe things that I knew were unbiblical and untrue. ... It is extremely difficult to leave the Mormon Church. Many will ask you what sin you have committed to 'lose your testimony.' They will encourage you to ignore your doubts, and to push them to the back of your mind, in order to keep your testimony." Post #5

*   *

Accusation – Guilt/Shame – "Not I, but you ..."

"I called the bishop and told him I was not returning to church, but other members continue to call me or come to my home. ... their arguments and my attitude towards them:

Argument: Aren't you going to honour the covenant made with God to keep the Sabbath?"

"Well, I was not aware I made this covenant ..."   Post #16 See: *Stage 1, 2 – 3, 4, 5, #16*

> *This is an extension of Stage 3 where "details" are left out and then later in stage 6 you are accused of having "chosen" them; therefore, you are "guilty" for not honoring a fraudulent contract.*

*   *

Guilt – Fear – Intimidation – Silence

"My husband and I left the church together, but I had more fear and more guilt about leaving that was related to what I had been taught about my being less valiant in the pre-existence and because of a special blessing to have our daughter."   Post # 37 *See: Stages 1, 2 – 3, 4, #37*

*   *

Guilt – Fear – Threats – Silence

"Until a person leaves Mormonism, they have no idea how painful it can be. When I left Mormonism (the last and final time) I was filled with fear and guilt. I was angry at a huge religion that had taken so much of my time, energy and money for so many years. I wrote my letter asking to be removed from the records of the church and was asked to come to what I call an exit interview. Actually it was a summons to my excommunication. I asked ... 'How can you excommunicate me when I already quit?'

"It is easy to rationalize the guilt out of a person's head, but difficult to get the fear out of your heart. Family can make it very difficult too. Mine has been pretty good, we just don't talk about it ..." Post #22 – 2

*   *

"Not I, but you ..." – Accusation – Reversal

"And if something can't be explained away, members are told to rely on faith. 'If we could explain everything then there would be no faith and without faith we couldn't be tested.'"   Post #30 *See: Stage 5, #30*

This not only belongs to stage 5 (Obfuscation) but stage 6, as well. Instead of the church doctrine being questionable, the situation was reversed and the one who had faith and believed (with no results) was being "tested." "It is not the church that is being tested, it is the member who is being tested." The problem disappeared through an emphasis on a misplaced accusation.

*   *

"Not I, but you ..."

"Mormons are so well trained to view any problem they may have with the church as their fault, since it could not possibly be the church's, that it is difficult to ever step out of that self-blame cycle. 'If I were just a better person, if I just had more faith, etc. etc. I would have peace, I would be happy, etc. etc.' Stepping out of the mind-set took me several years."　Post # 42　*See: Stage 5, #42*

The Church's stance on this is that the Church is perfect ... the individual is not. The Church projects its own guilt to faithful, obedient, individual members ... (who have been subjected to repeated double-binds creating unearned guilt) ... who are then blamed and disowned ("Not we, but you" are guilty) ... which invalidates the outward claim of their own positive, virtuous assessment of Mormonism, "By their fruits they shall be known."

*   *

"Not I, but you ..."

"But the anxiety and panic whenever I would go to church would continue. I thought it must be God's way of telling me I didn't belong. The Bishop would insist that perhaps I wasn't 'doing my part' by reading the Book of Mormon. That I should study it more diligently. God would give me comfort if I TRULY sought it ... I finally told the Bishop about my experience with the counselor in the Bishopric between the ages of 7 and 8. (*Before and after baptism, he had sexually abused her.*) He immediately got a cold look on his face and shut off completely. He told me right then that he was unable to help me any further and that he wouldn't be able to speak to me again until I got professional help."　Post #61 *See: Stages 4, 5, #61*

When her problems didn't directly involve the church she was innocent, and for relieving her distress only the reading of the Book of Mormon was given as remedy. She was accused of not "doing her part," and of not TRULY seeking to be comforted, because if she really wanted comfort she would study more diligently. Each step of the way her unearned guilt was compounded. When he found out that her problem directly involved a counselor in the Bishopric it became, "Not the church, but you are mentally ill. You need psychiatric help." This is a classic reversal when the church is confronted with facts against its leaders. Instead of the counselor being advised to get psychiatric help, the victim, by silent consent, is no longer innocent but, judged "guilty" and labeled "mentally ill." Mormonism causes the problem, seeks to cure it by the use of the same means that caused it, then if the member isn't "cured," it is the victim who is mentally ill, not the church leaders or the doctrine.

Experiences by Men – Stage 6

Demonized – Intimidation

"We officially left the church in March of 1994 through a letter requesting our names be removed from the church records. Since that time, in all too typical mind control like fashion, members of the church have avoided us. The Regional Representative even came up from Alabama and spoke out against us in a Sacrament meeting three weeks after we left and told the members that if they ever talk to us or if we give them materials, they are to contact their Bishop. Only an organization that had something to hide would be paranoid about the truth being revealed about itself. It is interesting that we would be considered such a threat. We had done nothing except request our names be removed from the records of the church. That was all. We learned that we really had few friends within Mormonism."

Threats

"The three bloody oaths that Mormons used to make in the temple and changed in 1990 ... appeared in the temple ceremony in the same order as in Masonry. In both cases (temple and Masonry) the first oath mentioned the slitting of the throat. The second spoke of the cutting open of the breast so that the heart and vitals could be removed and the third mentioned disembowelment. In all three cases the same penalties were demonstrated." Post #1 *See: Stage 5, #1*

*   *

Accusations – Threats – Intimidation – Invasion of Privacy

"I called the local bishop and asked him to forward a letter to Salt Lake City, Utah. In that letter I stated that I wanted my name removed from the records of the Church. He sounded very distressed ... He asked me if I had sinned against the Church, and, if I had, that I must go through a bishop's court. In this court I'd be judged as to whether I warranted excommunication, in other words, cut from the Church on their terms. I told him that I wouldn't attend any court because I no longer recognized his authority. ... About two weeks later, I was away for the evening. ... the bishop had come over ... He told (*his wife*) all the horrible things that would happen to me in the afterlife if I continued with this process ... The only reason he was there was to get my phone number (it's unlisted). I clearly told him I wasn't to be contacted at home, and he disregarded my wishes.

"About two months passed without any progress. I received a phone call one evening from the bishop. ... asked me to meet with him ... I asked him what he wanted to talk to me about. ... He said the Lord had a calling for me. I told him I wasn't an active member and wasn't interested. He turned nasty then, mocking my voice and started pronouncing doom on my head if I refused the Lord. I hung up the phone." Post #2 *See: Stages 2 – 3, 4, 5, #2*

*   *

Intimidation – Invasion of Privacy

"I received a telephone call ... informing me that the Stake President wished to meet with me. I was curious why but had no reason to suspect anything other than the standard reasons ... I arrived at the Stake President's office ... I saw that my bishop was there with him ... (*It was*) suggested that we kneel for a prayer, which I agreed to ... there was an envelope on his desk from the office of the Seventy in Salt Lake City. The Stake President opened the envelope, and said, 'I have received some disturbing information from Elder Glen L. Pace, indicating that you have been publishing anti-Mormon material on the Internet. Is this true?' I asked to see the material. Included in the packet were two esoteric essays on epistemology and historicity, neither of which was derogatory, nor which could be considered heretical or antithetical to the LDS Church. Also included was an article from the San Francisco Chronicle (an interview with Pres. Gordon B. Hinckley, along with the author's conclusions), and, the piece de resistance, a printout of a private email thread between myself and an ex-member, who is now part of a Fundamentalist group in Manti, Utah. Our correspondence, by the way, consisted of a bit of bantering, questioning, and the exchange of ideas. We parted company amicably several months ago.

"...When I asked how the email was obtained, the SP indicated that he didn't know and that the request to investigate me had come from Elder Pace. At that point, I became absolutely livid. I felt extremely violated. To realize that not only was a private conversation being used against me but that Church leaders would willingly comply with what was such an obvious ethical outrage has inspired a whole flood of emotions – anger, resentment, hurt, feelings of violation, and so on. I expressed my outrage at the SP and the Bishop, and, when asked about whether or not I believed in the Church, I responded that that was not the point – the point was that the information which would lead them to question my personal beliefs was obtained unethically, and was, therefore, not subject to discussion.

(Part of the letter he sent to his Bishop) ... "The use of private, personal correspondence in a Church investigation is, as I clearly expressed, a violation of my privacy, and highly unethical. In addition, the accusation that I personally published 'anti-Mormon' material, ascribing to me an article published in the San Francisco Chronicle and comments on it by my correspondent is not only incorrect, but shows the extremes to which the totalitarian mentality which inspired this inquisition will go."   Post #7

*   *

"You Chose"

"The first time I personally ever had doubts was when I went to the temple for the first time in the 1980s. The whole concept of the temple was a great thing I thought at the time. Here I could be sealed to my family forever. Here I could help others who never had a chance to receive 'ordinances' necessary for salvation receive them. When I actually went through to get my own endowment however, I was horrified by what went on, but I didn't say anything – similar to many Mormons. Not only was there nothing spiritual about the experience, the way the endowment is presented smells of cultism. You are instructed early on in the endowment that you can withdraw rather than go through the ceremony. Of course no one withdraws because you have no idea what is going to happen; you have your family and friends all sitting around you, and nothing has happened yet to incline anyone to withdraw. The next thing you know, you have taken a series of vows in unison with everyone else which hardly resemble anything you normally do in your LDS experience. Before 1990, you also had extreme penalties or 'bloody oaths' associated with the violation of any of these vows." Post #12

> *From stage 1 to stage 5 members are fed only "milk" ... Families are forever, Eternal marriage, Baptism for the Dead, etc. Once inside the temple and having experienced the preliminaries ... still with "milk" as your understanding, you are asked whether or not you want to proceed or withdraw ... with no explanation. You have no reason to object; you agree, en masse, with the rest of the Flock. When you find out that you were given "meat" for which you were not prepared, you find that you "chose" without having a choice. This is a repeat of stage 3; you thought you were agreeing with "milk" and that that was all there was to it. When this deception isn't seen, members will believe that they really chose, rather than that they had been manipulated.*

* *

Fear – Shame – "Not I, but you ..."

"At this point, the reader may ask, 'If you didn't believe in what you were doing, why didn't you quit?' ... As a Mormon, one is expected to do certain things and is taught that doubts arise from Satan. I just figured that there was some inner failing on my part that kept me from seeing 'the emperor's new clothes,' and that one day, if I was truly 'worthy,' I would be able to truly feel that which everyone around me seemed to feel. Until that time, my mind-set was one of waiting."

Accusation – Guilt/Shame

(An Ecuadorian convert's child had died) ... "We *(the missionaries)* did not see him for several weeks. When we finally did run into them *(the parents),* they avoided eye contact with us and quickly begged off. A night or two later, this man walked up, staggering drunk, apologizing to us for his weakness and lack of faith. He felt that God was punishing him for his sins and that he deserved the loss of his child. He went on to explain that he was once a member of the Otavalo Tribe of Indians – they are a reasonably pure strain of ancient natives from Inca times. They are extremely clannish, and are not allowed to marry anyone outside of the tribe. He met and fell in love with his future wife, who was not of this tribe, when he was on a trip to another town. When he took her home to tell his family of their intentions, he was told that if he was to pursue this course, he would be completely cut off from his family, and it would be as if he had never been born. Following his heart, he ignored their threats, and married the woman. He related how their life had been difficult ever since because he did not do as he was told, and the death of his child was further proof of his sins. He clung to us, sobbing for our forgiveness.

"My companion derided him for being drunk, and I walked away from the spectacle, unable to give any comfort to this man's grief, and angry with my companion for being such a hypocritical ass." Post #19 *See: Stages 2 – 3, 4, 5, #19*

> *This missionary companion had been dehumanized. The native Indian, the individual who was suffering as a human being, was not being recognized; he had not yet been dehumanized ... and that was not acceptable. Only his Dis-Obedience to the Binder took priority; he had gotten drunk in order to relieve his "irrelevant" pain ... he had broken the taboo contained in the Word of Wisdom ... for that, he "deserved" to be shamed.*

> *This is an example of tribal mentality. He was an outcast for marrying outside his own clan ... Mormonism does the same in that if you are not married in the temple, you will be excluded from your family's clan and tribe in* this *life and the* next. *This man had become an outcast from* two primitive tribes.

*   *

Accusation – Guilt/Shame – Demonized – An Outcast

"After three months in Sweden, I had tried to convince them (*his parents)* in tapes and in letters that I'd made a mistake going on a mission, and that I'd like to come home, but their startled reactions – emotional letters to the mission president imploring his patience, and tapes and letters to me entreating me to reconsider, caused me to abandon my pleas. They – my father in particular – had pinned much of their hopes for eternal salvation as well as an improved earthly life for themselves and our family on my completing my mission.

(He quotes from "Under the Prophet in Utah" ...)

"After he has taken his vows as a priest, how shall he dare to violate them? He knows that if he loses his faith on a mission – in other words, if he dares to make any inquiry into the authenticity of the mission which he is performing – he becomes a deserter from God in the very ranks of battle. He knows that he will be held forever in dishonor among his people; that he will be looked upon as one worse than dead; that he will ruin his own life and despoil his parents of all their eternal comfort and their hope in him." From, "Under the Prophet in Utah," Frank J. Cannon and Harvey J. O'Higgins. Post #23 *See: Stage 5, #23*

*   *

Fear – An Outcast

"It has been difficult to get past the idea that if I'm wrong *(about leaving the church),* my eternal salvation is at risk. It has been difficult as I have watched my friends walk away." Post #27

*   *

Accusation – Guilt/Shame – Demonized

"Mormon sex counselors. It was at this point that I started to realize that my Bishop was nothing more than an Elder of the Mormon Church taking his turn at being the Bishop. He didn't really seem to be in tune with God-relaying divine guidance to me through his priesthood as the church taught. The best advise the Bishop could give was to hum a hymn the next time I felt sexual temptation come my way. ... Hum a hymn? It certainly didn't work.

... I expected the meetings with my bishop to be compassionate and reassuring. It was more like an IRS audit. I prayed endlessly to be delivered from those temptations. I felt that there was something wrong with ME. I prayed to be healed of this 'affliction.' I beat my fists into my pillow in agony. I used every ounce of faith I could muster to overcome this problem. I was puzzled as to why I could not control these natural urges via faith. The church taught that the Holy Spirit could protect you from temptation. With the Holy Spirit and faith, you could cast off the 'natural man.' 'Lead me not into temptation, but deliver me from evil' just didn't seem to be working with me. Of course, I blamed it on myself and thought there was something wrong with me. I thought I was perverted. I felt evil inside. I hated myself." Post #28 *See: Stages 1, 2 – 3, 4, 5, #28*

> *The two most basic needs of the human species are sex and survival. Mormonism controls both. Members of the church are dehumanized as to their own needs. Sex is to be 'used' in the 'service' of the church, which means, 'for procreation only' ... for the survival of the church. The more births inside the church, the faster its growth. Personal, honorable expression of sex is 'evil.' There is no personal ownership of one's body in Mormonism; it belongs to the Binder. Each step of The Pattern creates more guilt and hatred against the Self and the human body. Yet, members are commanded to 'love thy neighbor, as thyself!' Where there is no love of Self, there can be no love for others! Mormonism kills what it professes to love. Again, this is the dual aspect of the Binder. What he "says" and what he "does" are two opposite things.*

*   *

Accusation – Guilt/Shame – Demonization

"I wrote down some thoughts about the Mormon perspective. This has helped me see why it is so difficult to leave the LDS Church. These points are all official doctrines of the Church and perspectives that are regularly ingrained into the membership:

(From his list:)

"Anything written by a former Mormon must be false or, at best, unreliable. Bottom line, you believe that former Mormons have evil intentions.

"Former Mormons leave the Church because of serious sin. Those who leave the Church in reality know that the Church is true and are liars just like the Book of Mormon Antichrists." Post #36 *See: Stage 5, #36*

*   *

Accusation – Guilt/Shame – "Not I, but you ..."

(After receiving his Patriarchal blessing and other blessings from his priesthood leaders, he believed in them and earnestly worked for the fulfillment of them. They did not materialize. When he questioned why, he was told ...)

"It was a mistake to believe that God would use you in a special way, above the way he was using your priesthood leaders." Post #38 *See: Stages 2 – 3, 4, 5, #38*

In the "milk" phase, members are told they are "special" and important. They look forward to the personal blessings given by the Priesthood leaders. They are also advised to pray for personal inspiration and guidance from the Lord. Each separate blessing implies that they are individuals, that what is promised to them (by "God," through God's Priesthood) is for them alone. Otherwise, why a personal blessing?

After faithfully applying all that he was taught, the blessings didn't happen. For an explanation, he received a reversal of the facts; instead of the blessings being for him alone, he was now accused of trying to be "special" ... that he shouldn't expect to be used any differently than his leaders. In other words, he was being told that "he shouldn't expect to be the center of the universe." In reality, the personal blessing was for him alone which he was to apply to his universe. The implication was that he was being "selfish," that he was intruding, in some way, on his leaders privileges. The fact of a personal, individual blessing was reversed to mean a "general" blessing, not a particular blessing. He was reduced from being an individual to a non-person within the general membership.

What was said was not what was done; the deceived became the "perpetrator" ... "Not we, but you" are "evil." Again, on the surface, Mormonism wants you to believe that you are still an individual, but when their Words fail, the disappointed one is accused of self-aggrandizement ... of even being above those who are above you ... self assertion becomes "aggression" against the members of the Flock; you became the exception; therefore, you are "guilty."

In short, "If the leaders can't have it, what makes you think that you can have it." Members must always step to the back of the line ... after the leaders ... "who will never lead you astray." The missing ingredient here is God's "Yes" promise, buried beneath all the "Buts."

*   *

Accusation – "Not I, but you ..."

"Today, I still attend church periodically with my wife and children. The bishop, my friends and my family know where I stand. I don't hide my beliefs from anyone who asks. I don't allow home teachers in my home because I'm tired of being treated like a sick patient by them."   Post #39

(This is a common accusation, "It is you who are mentally ill, not us.")

*   *

Zig-Zag – Threats – Intimidation

Zig: "The bishop called me in for an interview just a few weeks ago. He told me he was inspired to call me as the gospel doctrine teacher for our ward. I declined and he of course asked me why. I repeated to him many of the questions that I have shared in this letter and he had no answers other than the standard cop outs that I refuse to accept, such as 'God's ways are not man's ways' and 'someday we will know the answers to these questions.' He cautioned me from doing too much critical thinking and said we had to 'live by faith alone.' I'm sorry, but if there is a god and he created me with my brain, I expect that he would expect me to use it.

Zag: "He then went on to threaten me with a disastrous event in my life or in the life of one of my family members that would bring me to my knees and back, weeping to the church if I didn't repent and come back willingly ... From concern to the lowest form of manipulation." Post #41

*   *

The Dual Personality

"... A solicitation in the form of a brochure, for a donation to my Alma Mater (BYU) ... With the background of smiling, clean cut faces (all of course from the four corners of the earth – the Church is very politically correct these days) was a "We are better than the World' type of quote of a past Prophet that pretty well typifies another Mormon attitude. By sending money to BYU, the brochure suggested I would help fulfill a prophecy that the Lord's university would far surpass other institutions of higher learning in all things temporal. Clearly, in addition to the persecution complex, Mormonism thrives on its feeling of superiority. ... The claims of Mormonism are serious. It is not a live and let live religion. It is dogmatic in its claims. Mormonism keeps its hold by suggesting that the elect will discount the assaults on logic and remain faithful. Obedience, worship, and sublimation of will are the earthly tests for eternal companionship with the Cosmic terrorist known as Elohim. Mormons are fighting for your eternal soul, and in the process, they cause many people to experience a loss in the richness of the here and now of this life." Post # 44 *See: Stage 5, #44*

*   *

Guilt/Shame – Fear – Threats – Intimidation

(His decision to leave the mission field through the regular channels:)

"The mission assistants ... tried to persuade me to stay. ... I couldn't explain all my doubts to them but simply told them I didn't believe, and I couldn't be a missionary any more. They didn't understand.

"We returned the next day because President Lee wanted to speak with me on the telephone. The missionaries that had been friendly and cajoling the day before were stone faced and tense. A definite wall had gone up between us. President Lee called ... He started with reminding me all that Jesus Christ had done for me, he lived and died for me – and now I was turning my back on him, and kicking dust in his face. That's what he kept saying over and over – that I was kicking dust in the face of Jesus Christ. That hurt – but what could I say?

"First, he said he would come right down. Then he wanted me to wait until Wednesday so he could give me a priesthood blessing. He asked me why I was leaving – and I told him. He didn't believe me – told me that that was just an excuse. Wanted to know why. He couldn't accept that I just didn't believe in what I was doing. He said that Satan had led my father away, and through my father was leading me away.

"He told me that I was making things worse. He warned me against planning on repenting later, that I was almost throwing away my chance to go to the Celestial Kingdom and become a God.

"... Events took a definite turn for the worse. He said 'It sounds like your mind is already made up – before you even talked to me.' I said 'I think it is President.' He then said something that still rings in my head – and will for a long time. 'Elder Hudson, by the authority of the Melchizedek Priesthood, and in the name of Jesus Christ, I command you not to leave the mission. And if you do, something will happen.' Stunned, I flatly said 'What?' (pause) 'I'm not telling you Elder, and I say it in the name of Jesus Christ, Amen.' Click ...

"My brain exploded and my soul cried out that this was wrong. This shouldn't be happening. The only thing this man of God had used to 'persuade' me to stay were guilt and fear. I told the assistants what had happened, and they were stunned. They said I must have misunderstood." Post #52

*   *

"Not I, but you ..."

"My companion and I had been teaching a black man the lessons. He happened to be married to a white LDS woman. We had an extremely good relationship with him. He was 'golden.'

"Well, one day we showed up to teach John and the mood was quite different. He was laughing and joking as usual but things seemed strained. John said that he had spoken with his mother about the church and that she had told him something ridiculous about the church. He was laughing like he could not even believe what she had told him. Well after a little prodding he came out and said that his mother had informed him that the church had not allowed blacks to hold the priesthood until 1978. He burst out laughing ... Then he must have seen the serious expressions on our faces. He stopped and asked if that wasn't the most ridiculous thing we had ever heard. Then we dropped the bomb and told him that this was indeed true. He began to cry out of anger and rage. 'When were you planning to mention this???' He asked. That phrase is still burned in my mind. Then he shouted 'I will never join a church that has been racist!' and left his own home in tears and we were left sitting on his couch with his now hysterical wife.

"My companion seemed to simply write it off by saying that John did not have the spirit or was unwilling to soften his heart to the spirit. ... We had no plan to ever discuss this doctrine with him. I talked to my mission president and accepted his explanation. ... it was something to do with 'God's ways are not the ways of man' and that 'after I died these things would be made clear to me.' Post #58 *See: Stage 2 – 3, #58*

*   *

"Not I, but you ..."

"Once I made my break with the church, I thought that I should not 'hide away.' On the contrary, I intended to meet with all of my Mormon friends, family and leaders ... answer their questions straightforwardly and bluntly. I wanted to accept their right to their own beliefs and would consider their views. I only hoped that in return my views might be treated with equal respect. This was quite naive on my part. All future communication 'elevated' itself to an official level and became a sort of 'one-way street.' They felt free to bear their testimony ... but responded angrily when I would bear mine. They crossed my beliefs and I respected their difference of opinion. When I stated my beliefs then 'I was trying to hurt people.'" Post #70 *See: Stage 4, #70*

Stage 7: Punishment – Punished for Being Punished

Compulsion/Subjection – Black is "White"

Helplessness – Depression – Abandonment

"Don't see this as Evil, see it as "Good"

In Stage 5 the "hook" was the word "Good." You were "Good" when you Obeyed the Binder's Words. In Stage 6 the "hook" was the word "Evil." You were "Evil" when you Dis-Obeyed His Words. In Stage 7 the "hook" is "Good/Evil," that is, the two become One ... as in the euphemism, when Black is disguised as "White." In biblical terms it is called the "Whited Sepulchre."

In other words, the dual personality of the Binder merges into One, he becomes both the Guardian and the Enforcer *at the same time*. Whereas, in the two previous Stages he alternated between the two, now he is the Punisher who punishes you for your own "Good." He says, "Don't see this as "Evil" (Black), see it as "Good" ("White").

In Stage 6 the member was blamed for having "chosen" the Binder's (fraudulent) Agreement (Stage 3) and then accused of not honoring it. That was the first punishment. When the member balks at this judgment, the Binder punishes again, to "help" the member see the error of his, or her, ways. This is the second punishment of Stage 7. As the "Good/Evil"-Guardian/Enforcer he is compelled to Warn, Command, and to Kill any mutinous thoughts or actions. The member either capitulates under fear and pressure and submits to the "Cure" which is more doses of the Cause (*The Pattern*) or stands firmly against the violation of the Self that is still alive. If the latter is the case, there is usually a curse of dire consequences pronounced against the member and he, or she, is cast out of the Flock and abandoned.

Since the whole *social structure of the church* ... with the rules of The Pattern governing it makes up *the members whole life and identity,* to be abandoned leaves the member without any means to cope outside the Flock.   Total Obedience resulted in total dependence on the Binder. Having lived totally in an Upside-Down world where only the Obedient can live in "peace" ... to be "cast out" into an unknown world where thought, experience, and independence is required, is not unlike the panic a small child feels when abandoned by his or her parents; they feel helpless. That analogy depicts the true state of this Stage. From Stage 5 to 7 the members have been admonished to become "as little children" ... to give themselves to the Binder, for He has promised not to lead them astray; He has been their Guardian, their Caretaker, even the Creator of their new identities. The outside world, they have been told, is the home of Satan and his Angels, and once there, they will be lost to their families who are still in the church ... forever.

The member who has been raped mentally, emotionally, and yes, physically (that is, loss of ownership of one's own body and in some cases literal rape), and who desires to leave, is punished again by the accusation that he is "trying to hurt others." The perpetrator has reversed the facts again, and returns back to bask in the adoration His Flock gives Him. The Flock continues to reflect His Guardian/Enforcer image by also turning their backs on the outcast. Those who rebelled and then submitted (repented) are afraid to stay and afraid to leave. They are trapped in another Double-Bind ... more depression sets in.

Helplessness – Compulsion/Submission – Abandonment – Depression

Black is "White" – Doubly Punished – "Don't see this as Punishment."

The Guardian/Enforcer

Experiences by Women – Stage 7

Abandonment – Doubly Punished

(This is the young woman – Post # 3 – whose husband was dying of brain cancer. She was his sole caretaker.)

"A man I knew as a teenager, in fact he was briefly a youth advisor/YM pres. when I joined was now (at the time of this story) the bishop of the ward I had been baptized into. For financial reasons (Oh, did I mention on top of everything else we were dirt poor??) I was considering moving closer to my parents' home so they could assist us a little bit with the care of our children. I had also hoped I could lean a little on the members of my former ward for help. But alas, it was not to be ... In a telephone conversation with the bishop (my ex-youth advisor) I mentioned that my husband was terminally ill and that I had two sons, both under age 5. I had naively asked if perhaps the RS would assist me in finding child care since it appeared that I was soon going to have to go to work to pay the bills. The bishop sounded cold and vaguely annoyed as he said 'The Relief Society is not a baby-sitting agency ...' Again, I was too hurt for words ... I am not a slacker and I never have been ... what I was asking for was an arrangement in which I could 'trade off' baby-sitting with another sister or something like that ... As my husband's condition worsened, a part of me continued to hope and pray for a miracle ... My husband endured endless blessings 'to be comforted': but no one had the courage to bless him to be healed. But wasn't healing supposed to be one of the signs that follow the True Church?"   Post #3 *See: Stages 1, 2 – 3, 6, #3*

In Stage 6 she had been accused (demonized) of being "lazy" for not being able to keep up her regular chores as housekeeper and mother of 2 children under 5, while having the added responsibility of being a full-time nurse to her terminally ill husband. This was termed a "character" flaw which the sisters felt they could not support. (See: Stage 6, #3) *The Society which was organized to bring "Relief" to those in need, especially Widows and Orphans, was now categorized as what it was not, a "baby-sitting agency"* (supposedly this was because she was not yet a widow). *She was placed in another Double-Bind. She was damned (by the Binder) if she couldn't earn enough money for the care of her husband, her children, plus a housekeeper (not to mention herself), without the means ... the training to find employment that would pay enough to make it all possible. She was also damned (by the Binder) if she stayed home ... (even though she had been taught, and trained in the church that "the woman's place is in the home.") ... because her house was always "messy" when the Relief Society "sisters" returned with her children ... one day a week. Here, the "Red Herring" of a "character flaw" replaced the facts ignored.*

   This was during the last year of her husband's life when he was virtually helpless. (This is another version of Stage 3.) *The emphasis is always on the trivial at the expense of the real human problem. She was being punished doubly. The promises the church had made were not fulfilled; the blame for these failures was projected to her, and now she is being punished for being blamed ... by being abandoned. She is now an outcast in the human world, where she is expected to take responsibility for herself and her own family, and not look to the church for "sympathy" or help because she has a "character" flaw. She is no longer a contributing working member of the Flock Family. She is now the "exception" ... the "individual" to be shunned.*

   Binders always punish with what they fear most ... abandonment and independence. They are the ones who most need others ... to feed them; it becomes a "life or death" matter for the Binder. For the Bound, if they have the courage to leave, it becomes possible for them to reclaim all the humanness that was stolen from them ... to live freely in the Real World which is the true home of all possibilities for understanding and love.

*   *

Abandonment – Fear

"Now, leaving the church didn't happen very dramatically. She (*her mother*) had no idea what was going on while I was away at college (*taking Christian foundation classes*) because I was afraid to tell her. I had a Mormon friend who left the church, and her family disowned her and kicked her out of the house when she was 16." Post #6 *See: Stage 5, #6*

*   *

Depression – Dire Consequences – The Cause is the Cure

"My inner depression was constant, and I sent home (*from her mission*) rambling letters expounding on my problems, 'how could I earn the peace of Christ,' and mentally debated the merits of suicide vs. admitting defeat and returning home. I once got on the train ... and traveled back to the mission headquarters to convince President Wheelwright to let me go home. He assigned me to his wife, and she took two days to convince me that if I went home, I was consigning myself to a lifetime of spiritual failure and inactivity within the church. Ironically, even though my devotion to the LDS faith had thus far only brought me depressions and low self-esteem, I still could not consider that perhaps the church itself was in err. I had built my adult life on the church, and the thought of leaving it was too frightening to contemplate. So I stayed on, alternating between resigned depression and inner pep-talks. When my mission finally ended, I flew home expecting life to get better, only to drop into another deep depression where I began to consider that there was no God at all (I could not yet conceive of a God outside the realm of Mormonism. God was so tied up in the church. He could not exist outside it). I was counseled by the stake president and told to have stronger faith and everything would work out." Post #42 *See: Stages 5, 6, #42*

*   *

Abandonment – Punished for Being Punished

"When I phoned the Bishop to tell him we were leaving the church and why, he was shocked, as well as everyone else. Bill told our Bishop & Stake President the reasons, but our search for truth meant nothing to them. ... The news quickly traveled through-out the ward after we left & the members were shocked. Our daughter was told at school that Bill must have committed adultery to leave the church and do this to his family. Another person told me that he was going through a mid-life crisis or probably was suffering from a chemical imbalance ... We attended our excommunication & that was difficult as we sat among what I thought were friends we had made over the course of many years. ... My bishop looked at me crying (along with some of the other brethren) & said there were so many wonderful things in the church & was it all so bad. I looked him in the eye & crying said, 'Bishop, I love my husband because I trust him, but if I found out that even though he treated me good 95% of the time, & was only unfaithful to me 5% in our marriage, the 95% of "wonderful" couldn't compensate for any percentage of deceit or a lie ... all the wonderful things mean nothing when you find out the whole thing is based on a lie.' ...

"No trial or event in my life could have prepared me emotionally for our exit out. The church leaders got wind of Bill & I speaking publicly in different churches about the falsehoods of Mormonism & why it is a cult. Our names were mentioned over the pulpit in the ward & for people to 'beware' of us. Our accounting firm that we had struggled to develop for over 5 years was gone in 2 weeks because our member clients were told to stay away from us. ... The children & Bill & I lost every one of our friends but more devastating than losing friends & our accounting firm was feeling betrayed by God. I felt forsaken and abandoned; if he loved little children so much, why did he allow me to be deceived by an organization when I tried to be so good and find truth.

"The whole experience in leaving was difficult for our children emotionally. We had just recovered a few years back from bankruptcy (a Mormon partner had stolen $40,000 from us & we had lost everything ... and now this mess.) Bill's side of the family offered little support since they were all 'devout' members of the church. With no job, no friends, no church 'home' anymore, the stress caused our oldest daughter to drop out of school her senior year & run away from home. Come to find out Bill's whole side of the family had 'rescued her' from her terrible fate & sent her to England without telling us a word. They justified their actions since we were 'apostates' & our misfortune of events was due to our own rebellion against the church.

"With no support anywhere I became extremely depressed. I shared with one minister who told me I was having a pity party & feeding my own pathology. His LACK of words of wisdom & compassion made my pain even worse because there was no where to go.   My parent's love and acceptance had been conditional my entire life, & now all my best friends in the church had abandoned me since I was no longer the 'perfect' Mormon with the 'happy active family' facade. Every day for several weeks I was absorbed with the thought of suicide to end my pain & nearly followed through with the plan to end my life.

(Even though her loss was great she writes...) "I have experienced a deep peace at the age of 40 that I never had before ... A member of the church told me they could never have done to our children what we did to ours because we put our family through hell. My reply was that I'd do it all over again because I value truth so much."   Post #48 *See: Stage 1, #48*

> *This couple was blamed for bringing all of their misfortunes onto themselves.   Their "sin" was that they thought they still had a free choice.   In leaving, they went against the church (the Binder), which made them "guilty" and "evil."   The hell they went through was deliberately caused by the members of the church, fulfilling their roles as reflectors of the Binder's mind in all things ... which means going against their "brother," "sister," mother, or father if either should leave the Flock.*
>
> *They were being punished for being punished. The first punishment was having been deceived.   Their second punishment was caused by their discovering it ... which resulted in their "apostasy"; therefore, they had "asked" for their own punishment! ...   An Upside-Down world of reversals.*

*   *

Abandoned – Punished for Being Punished – Fear – Silence

"I would try and call him (the bishop) at home and he would refuse my calls. (My calls were always a priority before.) ... *(before she had told him about being molested by a counselor in the bishopric, in a church building, when she was a child.)* I felt abandoned again. I felt alone and discarded and violated. I had shared things with this Bishop that I hadn't shared with anyone and he just plain didn't care anymore. I was suicidal. I didn't believe that God could or would love me if His Bishop couldn't love and accept me. I truly believed that with all of my heart.

"In the meantime, my husband watched me struggle through a suicide attempt and loss of faith in my Church and myself. It was at this time that the old bishop was replaced by a new one and I felt encouraged to seek his help. Perhaps things would be different. Well, they weren't. Not even close. I felt disfellowshipped. We had no home teachers, no visiting teachers. And since we had no family around us ... I felt so alone.

"My husband and I became disillusioned with what we had been reading and the experiences we had gone through. We wrote the bishop a letter asking that our names be removed from the records of the church.

"We have suffered so much. I feel I've lost my identity, my God, my legacy, my heritage, my family's respect, etc. I wrote to my Grandpa on April 23, 1993 telling him of my decision to leave the church and why. (I left out the sexual abuse parts.) My grandfather was the only person in my life that I felt loved me unconditionally. He never responded to my letter. When we would talk by telephone, it was as if my letter never was sent. ... I asked him at one point if he read the letter, and he told me he did, but that's all that was said. I know he was disappointed. He told me that he knew I'd come back when I figured things out. Three months to the day I sent that letter ... my grandpa died. So did a major part of me. I flew back to Utah for the funeral. My Grandmother (even though she knew I had left the church) asked me to speak. I did. It was hard, but so joyous to be able to share my thoughts and feelings about my beloved friend, mentor, father, grandfather. The only rough spot was my Grandmother telling me that my grandpa was disappointed with my decision to leave the church and felt that I had turned my back on the Lord. This made me angry. I never turned my back on the Lord. (Did I?) Wasn't he the one who turned his back on ME? What my Grandmother said to me hurt me more than if she had slapped me as hard as she could." Post #61 *See: Stages 4, 5, 6, #61*

> *Binders, and those who reflect the Binder's Mind, take away from others what means the most to them ... where it would hurt the most; the devastation must be total; all members must "die before they die," "voluntarily," or by*

force. This subliminal message, not infrequently, leads to suicide. Again, this is a tribal mentality.

Experiences by Men – Stage 7

Punished for Being Punished – Dehumanized

"The treatment I received from both mission presidents was completely unwarranted. I am sure that the fact that I was seriously ill, and making an issue of receiving proper treatment, made them think that I was something less than a dedicated missionary. Their whole attitude was one of annoyance, and I was treated with disdain as a result of their mind-set." Post #19 *See: Stages 2 – 3, 4, 5, 6, #19*

*   *

Abandonment – Punished for Being Punished – Fear

"My companion and I were expelled from Sweden in December 1960 for sharing a Thanksgiving dinner 'out of district' with Elders in a neighboring town. I had long since abandoned the idea of leaving my mission early because I felt an obligation to my parents. My companion and I were sent back to the States on separate flights. As my plane crossed the Atlantic I felt like a condemned man. Or worse, since I was convinced that I was bound to become a Son of Perdition. I remember trying to console myself with the thought (from the 'Journal of Discourses' that there was only going to be a handful of souls whose sins would merit eternal damnation, but I was certain (otherwise why such despair?) I was destined to join that handful cast into dark and everlasting space with our unexpiated sins forever weighing on our souls. The Swedish Mission President, Gideon Omer, hurled wrathful prophecies at me on the eve of my departure, ... one of his prophesies was inspired by a rumor he'd picked up from his Traveling Elders – the mission 'inquisitors' – that along with being 'head strong,' I had aspirations to be a writer. 'I prophesy,' he thundered   ... 'in my capacity as president and prophet of this mission, that you will never publish a line.' *(Which proved not to be true.)*

"After I arrived in Georgia I lost, for several months to follow, my ability to enjoy the taste of food, or to appreciate music, or see a movie without assuming for myself the guilt that should have been reserved for the villain. Even a Walt Disney movie like '101 Dalmatians' tapped feelings of fear and loathing." Post #23 *See: Stages 5, 6, #23*

*   *

Depression

"By the end of my mission I was heart-broken and emotionally exhausted. It seemed that God had failed me or that I had failed God. I could not understand what had gone wrong. I remember jogging one day after my mission, thinking, 'It sure seems like God aims to confuse me.'

"At this time my prayers changed. I would weep in despair, or I would ask God to take my life. I said that if I wasn't going to know Him, that I would rather simply be dead. After the end of my mission I never again told anyone I knew the gospel was true.

"I did not kill myself, however, as I believed it was wrong to do so." Post # 38 *See: Stages 2 – 3, 4, 5, 6, #38*

*   *

Outcast

"My father was unprepared for my concerns. ... I gave him the reasons I could not believe, starting with masonry and ending with the Book of Mormon ... He talked to his bishop (who is also a professor of ancient scripture at BYU), consulted a Mormonism CD-ROM and read Sorenson's faith-first-aid-kit. That – and social pressure to be a pillar of faith for the rest of the family – was enough to convince him that I had fallen prey to the pride of my intellect and the deceiving of Satan. When he broke the news to the rest of the family (I was not present), he read to them 2 Nephi 9:28 – 29: 'O the vainness, and the frailties, and the foolishness of men! When they are learned they think they are wise, and they hearken not unto the counsel of God, for they set it aside, supposing they know of themselves, wherefore, their wisdom is foolishness and it profiteth them not.' That is what he thinks of my reasoning and my decision to act as I believe." Post #63 *See: Stages 2 – 3, #63*

*   *

Black is "White" – Helplessness – The Shepherd and the Enforcer

"It's a difficult matter to explain to people the degree of psychological harm that can be done by such an organization (the Mormon church) because of its powerful influence and indoctrination asserted on unknowing children. Fear of eternal failure and separation from one's family are the most common tools used by the church to keep people in line. This is so effective on many people who were raised in Mormonism as children because it play's on a child's sense of dependency on his or her parents and community, causing a sense of separation anxiety at the thought of going against the system. In fact, it's almost unimaginable. This is overlaid with messages of Christian ethics and Godly love for us and our well-being. A sense of feeling good and 'knowing' the church is true was set up all around me. It was as though awful consequences and fear was laid out in front of me, then in the same breath everything I needed to do in order to stay good with God were offered as antidotes. This is the very situation upon which I base my belief that Mormonism doesn't know the meaning of unconditional love and acceptance, some of the most important needs a child must experience in order to feel free and well adjusted as an adult." Post #65

*   *

Black is "White"

"One last reflection upon my recent 'interview' with the Stake President. There is in the Church Office Building, an Orwellian organ of image maintenance called the 'Strengthening the Members Committee.' Staffed by two members of the Quorum of the Twelve, this committee keeps clip files on critics of the church, as well as members of the church who express public criticism of the church in either printed or spoken form. Files on members are made available to local leaders (Bishops, Branch Presidents, and Stake Presidents), who then may 'counsel' or discipline the members as they see fit – although, in some recent cases (that is, that of historian Michael Quinn), members of the Quorum of the Twelve have taken personal interest in a particular disciplinary outcome.

"It was made plain to me in the course of my interview that the Church has kept a file on me for at least three years."   Post #64
See: Stage 5, #64

> *Note: President Hinckley admitted to this church procedure during a (September 8, 1998) Larry King Live interview.   Genealogical records can be used to collect information about past and current individuals. Hinckley said to King, "If you would like to know about LARRY KING LIVE we'd probably have a record on you." King replied, "I know you have a record on my wife because I married a Mormon, it should be stated." Hinckley: "We have them on not only those in the church, but out of the church as well."*

*   *

A Wall as Abandonment

(After leaving the church and trying to establish two way communication with Mormons, only a one-way communication was acceptable to them.)

"An interesting thing happened at this point: a new wall of formal politeness appeared on my next encounter.   No real communication ... no genuine questions ... no attempt to bring me back. Lots of silence. Real fear in the eyes of some. Often, I felt as though I was invisible.

"After a good deal of time I can now accept this wall and understand it. An active Mormon needs this wall ... and they fear and resent every effort on my part to dismantle even a single stone. I am not speaking here of the dismantling of their religion, but of dismantling the wall between us ... the wall between our relationship. Although I accept it, I cannot endure such one-way conversations. I need real communication or no communication at all ... and so have found the only solution on my part is to support the wall ... keep it in place."   Post #70 *See: Stages 4, 6, #70*

Stage 8: Bound – Love/Hate

Brain-washed – "Voluntary" Union

Stage 8 is the culmination of all the previous stages and the possible successful resolution of the Binder's Double-Bind reversal in Stage 4. It is at this stage that the "Black Hole" of depression sets in. The member either "accepts" the Binder's punishments as being "deserved," that is, that he or she believes that they had "asked for it" through their "disobedience," and completely merges with the Binder's mind, losing what self-identity they had left, or through a spark of life for survival not completely extinguished, escapes from the Binder. In this case, the person has escaped physically from the environment but still has the conditioned mind implanted by the Binder; the mental Pattern of unearned guilt is taken with the Bound. However, to leave the direct influence of The Pattern is the first and biggest step to freedom.

Those who stay become completely brain-washed and become One with the Binder ... inseparably Bound. Since the entrance into the Binder's Celestial Kingdom is through the death of the human body, the Bound yearns to die ... to be released from this earthly "veil of tears." This is a reflection of the Binder's underlying Pattern of death.

The Binder makes life on earth a literal Hell, then promises a "life" of Heavenly Joy in the Hereafter; death is the "cure" of all ills and the escape from the "Bottomless Pit," or "Black Hole." The carrot on the stick, the original promise of Stage 2, is held out even to the end ... "Ye are *bound* when ye do what I *say*, but when ye do not what I *say*, ye have no *promise*." However, as the Double-Bind is constituted, the Bound one can never completely please the Binder and is always a failure through not having done what the Binder commands "perfectly." You "must endure to the end" (be "tested") without the knowledge that you will be judged worthy enough to receive what you have worked for all of your life. This will only be known at the final judgment bar. "Yes," man *is* that he might have joy, "But," not in *this* life. By this time, the investment in Mormonism has been so total that it would be a form of "death" to walk away "penniless" from it. Those that stay are the "walking dead" clinging blindly to the rod that holds the unattainable promise forever just beyond their reach.

To recapitulate The Pattern's Double-Bind evolution to this point:

Stage 4 The Double-Bind established what was the "Good," and what was the "Evil."

- What is **"Good"** is what is *for* the Binder.

- What is **"Evil"** is what is *for* the individual Self and therefore, *against* the Binder.

- The function of the Double-Bind is to instill unearned, inescapable "Guilt."

Stage 5 Good: Praise is given when the "Good" is supported, when all "choices" are *for,* and in obedience to, the Binder. *(Zig)*

Stage 6 Evil: Accusations are hurled at the "disobedient" for supporting the individual Self, who is now labeled "Evil." *(Zag)*

Stage 7 Good/Evil: "Good" *and* "Evil" are *reduced (fused)* into One. You are punished for your own "Good," so "Don't see this as "Evil." Punishment equates to *"Love."* The Binder *chastises* those He *"Loves." (Zig/Zag)* This is the preparatory stage for Stage 8 via *coercion and force.*

Stage 8 Love/Hate: The extension of "Good" and "Evil" reduced to One (Stage 7) ... *as the product of "Love"* ... is the essence of the "Love/Hate" relationship in Stage 8. The difference being that "Love" in Stage 7 was compulsory through milk labels and coercion. In Stage 8 it becomes the *"Voluntary,"* brainwashed Union of the Bound to the Binder. This Union is experienced as a *"dark cloud"* above the mind of reason and is the aim of the *"simplification,"* the *"reductionism"* of stage 7. All is reduced to the Binder's dual mind-set which is now fused as One, a "Love/Hate," "Good/Evil" personality. The Bound is to "Love" what she/he "Hates" (the Binder), and "Hate" what is Loved (the Self). This hatred of Self (in Stage 8) that can still be felt (because the Self is not *totally* dead), and the consequent "Guilt" that this lack of personal *integrity* causes, deepens further the depression that has previously been instilled.

This is the stage of the "Voluntary" *loss of Identity*. Desires for complete annihilation arise ... total obliteration of the Self is the goal. However, the last Double-Bind usually stops these suicidal thoughts. You would be damned if you took your own life. And, you would be damned if you didn't, because the Binder forbids the taking of your own life. Your life doesn't belong to you any longer. Being totally Bound and dependent on the Binder for your means of survival, the Bound believes he/she would be damned (would die) *if they did* leave Him, and on the other hand, they feel they would be damned (would also die) *if they didn't* leave Him, because they would be subjected to the continuation of a life of pathological mental and emotional pain. However, the Binder doesn't want the Bound dead ... yet; that is why it is "forbidden." The Bound must be "tried" as to whether they can "endure to the end." The Pattern of the Double-Bind is the road to this "perfection" ... the *perfect* "death" designed by the Binder. The Binder holds the "keys" of Life *and* Death, the ultimate Dictator of both.

The irony here is that the more the member hates him/herself, the less he/she is able to love. The possibility of love has turned to fear of what one is commanded to love. The means for the ability to love is taken away, and *at the same time*, the Binder commands that He be loved with ALL of one's *personal* heart, mind, and soul which has been systematically deadened ... *"reduced,"* and *"simplified"* ... into the *"generalization"* of the One Mind. You become the projection of his fused, "Love/Hate" mind. The Binder kills what he professes to love but still demands to be loved by those whom he has incapacitated. *Madness!!*

The Black Hole of Depression – Unawareness of the Cause
Love/Hate – "Voluntary" Union

Brain-Washed – Loss of Identity

Experiences by Men – Stage 8

Depression – Unawareness of the Cause

"Ever since I can remember, Mormonism just didn't seem right to me. .... These feelings continued to grow as I did. ... I knew that a mission was out of the question, because I didn't believe. Yet, I didn't know why. ... Seeing everyone believing and content just pushed me further into depression and confusion."   Post #2 *See: Stage 2 – 3, 4, 5, 6, #2*

> *The Pattern is insidious ... and because of our trust and inexperience we are not aware of its infiltration into our minds. Guilt from the Double-Binds, plus our unknowing state of mind, causes confusion and depression; a "cloud of unknowing" hovers over the brain.*

*   *

Loss of Identity

"So much of my identity was tied to the church. I half expected to become invisible if I ever decided to leave."   Post #4 *See: Stage 5, #4*

*   *

Loss of Identity

"I view the years I spent as a Mormon as a kind of mindrape. Mormonism gave me a terrible self-image (I could not live up to the impossible, 'perfect' expectations) ..."   Post #10 *See: Stage 2 – 3, #10*

*   *

Loss of Identity – Unawareness of the Cause

"That place (*the Language Training Center*) is a serious boot camp for removing a person's individuality, and replacing it with an automatonlike mentality that leaves the weak minded completely gutted emotionally. Not unlike a military boot camp, the LTM drains a person of their roots, and bonds them to a system of religious salesmanship that makes them feel justified in doing just about anything for the cause, and walk around with a false sense of invulnerability.

"For some reason that I cannot fully fathom, the Mormon church did not provide that which I needed in order to be spiritually fulfilled."   Post #19   *See: Stages 2 – 3, 4, 5, 6, 7, #19*

*   *

Unawareness of the Cause

"I'm not quite sure why I left the church. ... It has been difficult to get past the idea that if I'm wrong, my eternal salvation is at risk." Post #27 *See: Stage 6, #27*

*   *

Unawareness of the Cause

"I've continued to struggle off-and-on with how I could have such strong beliefs that the LDS church is false yet still have the Church continually on my mind."   Post #36 *See: Stages 5, 6, #36*

*   *

Depression – Despair

"... I had been brought to a point of great spiritual despair. At least McConkie will come to my aid, for apparently I was not alone. He says, 'In some instances it leads to despondency.'"   Post #38 *See: Stages 2 – 3, 4, 5, 6, 7, #38*

> *His despondency was regarding a personal relationship with Christ which he had previously been advised to establish, but which afterwards was rescinded, and then was blamed for having listened to, and believing in his leaders in the first place. "Yes" was, "But" now ... "No," then, "Not I, but you" are in the wrong."*

*   *

Crisis of Awareness

"What I can no longer accept is intellectual suicide, period."   Post #39 *See: Stage 6, #39*

*   *

Love/Hate – Love the Lie – Hate the Truth – Depression

"The more I read from the church history, the worse I felt. The more I studied, thought and prayed, the more problems I found with the church and what it claimed to be. I started compiling a list of problems. It became harder and harder for me to go out and teach. When I got to the part of a lesson where I had to bear my testimony (even memorized in Navajo), my stomach would tighten into a knot. I became physically ill and couldn't go out to teach. ... Finally, I realized that I couldn't do it anymore – tell people that I knew the church was true when I had such serious doubts. I felt like I was in a fog, and I didn't know what to do. ... The most important lesson I learned from the LDS church is that living a lie is actually a slow, painful spiritual death. It is much better to face the truth and live."   Post #52 *See: Stage 6, #52*

*   *

Love/Hate

"The BYU Honor Code Office likes to describe itself as an agency that is loving and caring, but the real reason it exists is to purge undesirable elements from BYU. (It always reminded me of how in Orwell's 1984, the Thought Police were headquartered in the Ministry of Love.)"   Post #57

*   *

Pathological Ignorance

"I don't know how my situation will resolve itself. I simply know that the LDS Church as an institution has a pathological inability to deal with the unadorned truth. I also know it is neither honest nor healthy to stuff my concerns into a 'little box' in my psyche and pretend as if I'm blessedly ignorant regarding many important things ..."   Post #64 *See: Stages 5, 7, #64*

*   *

Loss of Identity – Unawareness of Cause

"I felt a vague sense that whatever I wanted, what I felt must be against God. I learned to alienate myself from myself. I learned to suppress my feelings, to shut myself down emotionally. That's perhaps the thing I'm most angry about now as I try to reconnect to myself, to repair all those years of psychic abuse and emotional neglect." Post #65 *See: Stage 7, #65*

* *

Despair – Love/Hate – Killing What it Professes to Love

"Again, how ironic it is that a church which begins by promising its members such joy and happiness actually causes them such worry and despair." Post #66 *See: Stage 5, #66*

* *

Brainwashing of Children – Adult Burdens Create the Loss of Childhood

"For my entire life I have been 'Mitch the miracle baby: Saved by God for a great and wondrous purpose. Lifted from the clutches of death by the hand of the Almighty Himself, to stand forth in these last days, and lead the armies of the saints against the forces of evil.' ... No one knows the burden I have carried because of this. No one knows the childhood night terrors I endured for something I never asked for. ... I was told that God had saved me above all others for a special purpose and that I now owed Him for it." Post #67

Experiences by Women – Stage 8

Brain-Washed – Loss of Identity

"The constant repetition of 'temple marriage,' and 'Saturday's warrior' and 'chastity' and 'every member a missionary' and 'you have the truth' really kept me together through my 'not so perfect' home life. I had deep underlying insecurities stemming from my parent's divorce and the poverty we lived in. I never worked through any of that till I left the church. I didn't have to think about who I was because I was told all the time who I was and what to do to have a happy life." Post #17

* *

Unawareness of the Cause

"I left Mormonism 10 years ago. ... Right now, it is as if I have a point at which I cannot think straight and to try to express my feelings is almost impossible. I reach the foggy state of mind that some have spoken of in their stories of leaving the LDS church." Post #22 – 3

* *

The Dark Cloud of Unknowing

As she began to study and question Mormonism: 'It was like this horrible dark cloud that had hovered over my head was lifted.'" Post #29 *See: Stage 5, #29*

* *

Depression – Thoughts of Suicide – Loss of Identity

"... the spiritual angst which haunted me my entire mission and also led me to consider suicide (which was not an option due to my conviction that God would be so angry at me for ending my life that my suffering would only continue in the next life). It saddens me to realize that throughout my entire journey in Mormonism I was surrounded by others suffering like me. We were all so well conditioned in Mormonism that we would not, could not, reveal our doubts to each other, so we all felt alone in our pain."

"I threw myself into church activity with such intensity and devotion that even my sister (who had encouraged me to join the church) was concerned over the complete change in my personality. In retrospect, it was really a loss of personality rather than a change. I no longer had any ideas or opinions of my own, every thought or belief I allowed myself had to be church approved." Post #42 *See: Stages 5, 6, 7, #42*

* *

Unawareness of the Cause

"It wasn't until after I left the church and starting living like a normal person that I realized how much the church had damaged my psyche." Post #43 *See: Stages 1, 4, 5, #43*

*   *

Depression

"One Sunday, a sister got up and spoke, ... Her entire talk was about her depression, and how her faith in the Savior had literally saved her, but that she still felt very little peace in her life, and constantly felt like she wasn't good enough. More than half of the sisters in the ward, including myself, told her how her talk affected them, and how they too suffered from depression, and felt empty and alone." Post #56

*   *

Unawareness of the Cause

"Though I felt at the time that I firmly believed all I was teaching, I have to admit that inwardly I would cringe when giving some of the concepts wondering how these people would ever believe what I was telling them. Somewhere inside, my brain was trying to get my attention, but I just was too programmed to listen." Post # 68 *See: Stages 1, 2 – 3, #68*

*   *

Love/Hate

"... the deeper I dug, the more rotten the foundation seemed, until I couldn't look away – or go back. And when I studied all of this, years after being inactive, I wanted to go back. I wanted the church to be true. But my heart ached with the suspicion we'd been lied to by Joseph Smith and church authorities following him." Post #69 *See: Stages 2 – 3, 4, 5, # 69*

This is the battered child syndrome. The battered child (or adult) will always want to go back to the batterer to be loved. The child feels guilty ... that it must be his or her fault that the Binder cannot love him or her.

Stage 9: Death/Suicide – Psychological Cannibalism

The prelude to suicide is accumulated, *unearned* "Guilt" and the *abandonment* by those in whom all of one's trust has been deposited ... the sense that one has failed in all things. Numbness sets in. One loses all feelings of sense perceptions, and feels nothing but a "Black Hole" of despair and the desire to die, the pain unendurable.

Mormonism fosters an unconscious death wish through The Pattern which is designed to destroy individual identity ... to lose oneself totally for the "upbuilding of the Kingdom of God on earth." The sincere devotee obeys the Law of Sacrifice of offering, literally, one's life and all of one's talents and possessions, if necessary, for the church. All of the words and promises by the leaders of the church have been believed and worked for diligently. Since the Gospel "plan" is based on fraud, that is, the Double-Bind, failure is a built-in result. The stronger the individual is, the more basic intelligence the member has, the more the pain and devastation one feels at the final failure. This person is labeled "mentally ill," a "misfit," and becomes the "exception" that can't be tolerated and is literally abandoned. Instead of help given, the member is accused of having committed some terrible sin, which reinforces the desire to die; the member is punished again ... for being punished.

Abandonment will be masked by "Not I (*we*), But, you, are evil." This member is abandoned in his or her most crucial time of need because he/she becomes a threat to the "Key" to "Salvation," the Double-Bind, and what it does. The member reveals a fact that gets too close to the poisonous source; the church is put on the spot with its own corruption of values that it must deny; it must have the *image* of "sanity," "joy," "happiness," "love," and, of course, "intelligence." Therefore, the member must be labeled the "enemy" of these "highest values." Mormonism *outwardly* fights what it *inwardly* is.

The victim is blamed and accused of needing "psychiatric" help; it is the member who is "mad," not the church. Or, church "psychologists" may recommend a drug of some kind (like Prozac) to "stabilize" a member by superficially erasing all of the anxiety that shows and indicates that something is radically wrong. The member is then able to continue his or her labors in the church uninterrupted. They need only to "read the Book of Mormon and the Doctrine and Covenants" and to "work harder to increase their faith." It is this "lack" of effort that has caused their "illness" they are told. In reality, it is just the opposite. The cause is prescribed as the cure which continues to destroy the ability to reason.

However, the underlying reasons for the depression are still there; the drugs merely put the problems back into the "little box" of denial that Mormonism had encouraged before the current outbreak; thus, the problems that caused the crisis are "forgotten." On the other hand, if the member is leaving, or has left the church (the real cause of the problem) and has sought help, certain calming drugs can elevate the desire to live and to give the energy necessary to probe the real cause of the depression. The problem once known and the Self Identity of the person re-established, the drug is no longer necessary. The chemical imbalance *caused by the anxiety inflicted by the Double-Bind Pattern* is restored to its balanced operating level. The brain is not separate from the body. What one thinks and feels affects the well-being of the rest of the body. Our sense perceptions and their normal chemical messages to the brain are our means of survival.

The major difference is whether a Band-Aid is used to cover a still festering abscess, or whether a fundamental cure is the goal. Without knowing the primary cause, there can be no real cure ... and an addiction to the drug results. At any time the desire to die could break through. Suicide is one of the "side effects" of the drug Prozac.

The church is the Whited Sepulchre which houses the living Dead. If this sounds grim, it is because the white-washed deadly falsehoods are being taken away, and what is left are facts that have been denied for too long. The problem needs to be identified, named and exposed. And, contrary to Mormon expectations, the factual truths can actually set us free.

We cannot fight or defend ourselves from the invisible. This is what Mormonism fears ... that we will objectify and identify the fraud. The very things the church considers its enemies are the very things that contain hidden realities which they want to keep hidden. Packer has identified three "major invasions" into the church, Gays and Lesbians, Feminists, and Scholars/Intellectuals.* In other words, Sex, the issue of choice in Procreating, and Reason. The other subject it fears, and which is carefully avoided, and rarely spoken of or defined ... considered too "sacred" to speak about ... is *Love*. Love is one of the "Mysteries of Godliness." In Mormonism, the "Mysteries" are not to be delved into; they belong to the *"next world."*

*   *   *

> *"The Truths which Science (Reason) reveals always surpass the dreams which it destroys."*
>
> ~ *Ernest Renan*

(Insertion, mine.)

---

* From "Talk to the All-Church Coordinating Council," May 18, 1993.

Death/Suicide – Psychological Cannibalism

The Life in Death and Death in Life Stage

Death of Love – Self-Loathing

Numb/Death of Feelings – Dumb/Death of the Mind

Experiences by Women – Stage 9

Suicidal

" ... I felt that I didn't even have the right to ask God for help. (You know – when you sin, the holy spirit is withdrawn from you!) I was consumed with thoughts of suicide daily ..."   Post #13 *See: Stages 1, 5, #13*

*   *

Empty of Self

"Because along with the freedom of the mind I was experiencing, was the fact that I no longer had anything to center me. I felt adrift in a black hole. A Mormon will tell you that this is the devil at work, 'come back to safety, come back to the light!' But I couldn't go back to that. ... I know now that I was lost because I had never learned to think on my own, to reason things out. I no longer had anyone telling me who I was or what my purpose in life was." Post # 17 *See: Stage 8, #17*

*   *

Death of the Mind

"I was so unhappy, but I did not believe I could ever be free from Mormonism. I thought I was doomed to struggle forever. ... I knew that I had given in to this life of anguish, but I would not, as a mother do the same to my child. I would not sentence him to this life of imprisonment. ... I didn't know all of the documentation that proves J.S. was a hoax and that the Mormons are still covering up the changes and the lies. I just knew that though I may struggle the rest of my life with the fear of their power over me, I would not, could not, sentence my innocent child to the same anguish. Does it ever get completely resolved? I still struggle, and I get so frightened of their power over my mind because I let them have such power at one time."   Post # 22 – 3 *See: Stage 8, #22 – 3*

*　　　*

Suicidal Thoughts

" ... now there was nothing to fall back on at all. I locked myself in my room and cried for hours at a time. Every day for several weeks I was absorbed with the thought of suicide to end my pain & nearly followed through with the plan to end my life." Post #48
See: Stages 1, 7, #48

*　　　*

Suicidal Thoughts

"Finally one night I was standing at my back door looking out at the beautiful snow while everyone else was asleep and contemplated suicide. I kept thinking, I should be happy, why aren't I happy, I must be doing something wrong, it's all my fault etc. etc." Post #53 *See: Stages 1, 2, 5, #53*

*　　　*

Numbing of the Mind – Perceptions still Alive

"I realize that I had been a prisoner of The Church of Jesus Christ of Latter-Day Saints ... I was terrified of the "great doom" that would come to me if I left the church. It tormented me for weeks, and into months. I finally decided that even though I didn't know why the church wasn't true, that because I felt in my heart that it wasn't true, that I should leave. It was the most frightening thing I have ever done in my life." Post # 55 *See: Stage 5, #55*

*　　　*

Depression – Fear of Death

"I'm certain that depression among women in the LDS church is rampant, and I feel that being free of the burden of constant pain and guilt will be one of the greatest accomplishments of my life. ... I felt for years that I was never good enough in God's eyes, and that I would never be perfect enough to return to him someday. I was constantly afraid of death, and what my fate would be on the other side. I no longer have that fear. Living my life in fear was hell!" Post #56

*　　　*

Suicide

"I also am personally aware of the oppressive environment the church imposes on others (especially the women) and how difficult it is to leave. I think that is reflected in Utah's well known high suicide rate."   Post # 59

*   *

Abandonment – Suicide

"I felt abandoned again. I felt alone and discarded and violated. I had shared things with this Bishop that I hadn't shared with anyone and he just plain didn't care anymore. I was suicidal. I didn't believe that God could or would love me if His Bishop couldn't love and accept me. I truly believed with all of my heart.

"In the meantime, my husband watched me struggle through a suicide attempt and loss of faith in my Church and myself."   Post #61 *See: Stages 4, 5, 6, 7, #61*

*   *

Difficulty in leaving Mormonism

"I almost got to the point of leaving the church but had no one to really talk to or no place to turn to. I did try a group of Christians who try to help those leaving the Mormon church but the person they sent to me had never been a Mormon and did not fully understand the difficulty in physically, emotionally and mentally leaving."   Post #68 *See: Stages 1, 2 – 3, 8, #68*

*   *

The Enemies of Mormonism – What is Done – Hate

"The LDS church claims to be led by men of God. They are supposed to receive direct revelation from Him. Yet this is a church that turns away from the needs of both its men and its women, a church that will not acknowledge the child abuse/incest that goes on between some of its members – abuse that destroys children and steals their childhood, that creates wounds they carry the rest of their lives. Women in the church – some women, by no means all – are just as scarred and scared, just as abused. Yet those in authority will not deal with these issues. Nor will they deal with women who feel it extremely unfair that they are still to be 'subservient' to their husbands, that they are not equal to their husbands, not even in the eyes of the LDS God. Mormonism is a patriarchy. For some, this is an acceptable way to live. For others, it's a torture chamber. Their treatment of homosexuals seeking help is appalling. While I am not gay, I was involved with a gay member of the church, and the hell he was put through – even as he begged for help – was appalling. Instead of self-acceptance for EVERY member, the church teaches conditional love ... To claim that it's God's will that people be hurt this way is emotionally, mentally and spiritually abusive."　　Post #69　See:　Stages 2 – 3, 4, 5, #69

Experiences by Men – Stage 9

What is *Said* – "Love"

"My faith was so seriously shaken by those first two years of college that I probably would have left the church or at least become inactive had it not been for Lowell Bennion. He said 'look, the important message of the church is love; it's main mission isn't proving that Joseph Smith was a prophet of God and that the Mormon church is the only true church on the face of the earth; it's about loving our fellow man and Christ. That has to be our highest priority at all times.' That made sense, he had given me a rationale for staying in the church." Post #4 *See: Stages 5, 8, #4*

*　　　*

The General (*One Mind fits All*) Vs the Individual – Totalitarianism Vs Personal Freedom

"The use of private, personal correspondence in a Church investigation is, as I clearly expressed, a violation of my privacy, and highly unethical. In addition, the accusation that I personally published 'anti-Mormon' material, ascribing to me an article published in the San Francisco Chronicle and comments on it by my correspondent is not only incorrect, but shows the extremes to which the totalitarian mentality which inspired this inquisition will go." Post #7 See: Stage 6, #7

Members commonly believe that the church agrees with the Constitution, and the Bill of Rights ... that they were divinely inspired ... that we each have equal rights, including the right to privacy. The 12th Article of Faith: "We believe in being subject to kings, presidents, rulers, and magistrates, in obeying, honoring, and sustaining the law." In Mormonism, what is said by the leaders and what is done are two different things; the leaders claim the right to privacy when it applies to themselves in defending themselves, but when it comes to individual members, they become "exceptions" to that rule of law. This kind of thinking is due to Mormonism's dual Theo-Democratic-basis ... a contradiction in terms, and the outcome of the dual personality of the Binder.

*   *

Brain-Washed

"I would agree, though, that the Missionary Training Center fits a lot of the standard criteria for brainwashing and 'cult'-type practices. In the MTC, free thought and free debate are strongly condemned, and contact with outsiders is strictly regulated. These are all traits common to so-called 'cults.'"   Post #18

*   *

Death of Mind and Perceptions

"I was somewhat offended by his *(the Mission President)* change in demeanor, and that he would try to manipulate me into doing something that may well have permanent negative consequences as far as my health was concerned. Mormon missionaries pay their own way, and I was no exception, so why should I be made to feel guilty because I didn't want to sacrifice my health, or even my life, for a 'cause' that I believed in only marginally? Keeping my composure, I reassured him that I had indeed prayed quite a lot regarding this matter, and that this was indeed the proper and only course of action. He questioned me once more on this, and I began to weary at his unwillingness to accept my decision about my life.

"Individuals placed in leadership positions often use their supposed superiority to manipulate individuals in their charge. Church members, especially missionaries, are taught that the leadership is 'inspired,' and that they should submit their decisions to the 'wise counsel' of those who are placed in stewardship over them. Philosophically, this is a bad thing, because it teaches people to question their own ability to make life decisions, and makes them more dependent upon the infrastructure of the church. The entire church organization is set up to make the membership feel commitment. Tithing, endless meetings, ward budget and other contributions, church jobs, and missions, are all designed to keep the membership dependent upon the organization. After all, how many people would want to give up membership in which they have invested so much of their time, money, and energy?"   Post #19 *See: Stages 2 – 3, 4, 5, 6, 7, #19*

This kind of treatment is due to the dehumanization of individuals in Mormonism. Only human beings can get sick; members are not allowed to be human ... to become physically ill. It implies they are "evil" in that they were not devout enough in their prayers and supplications ... lacked "faith" to remain "well."

This is similar to the experience of Post #38 in regard to prayer. It contains another Double-Bind. As with the young man in Post #38 when he was asked to pray for guidance, the implication was that he could expect personal guidance and answers to his prayers. When his prayers and his blessings from priesthood leaders were not answered, nor shown, or, in the case above where this missionary had received an answer, but it was "unacceptable," they were both judged "guilty" for expecting to be "special" ... "exceptions." They were damned if they did pray, and they were damned if they didn't pray. "Yes/" pray, "But" ... why do you think you are so "special" to receive a personal answer ... one way or the other. (The personal Vs the general ... the individual outside the tribal "oneness.")

Mormonism consistently kills what it claims to love ... the personal. The Binder, as "Guardian," 'loves,' and at the same time, the Binder as "Enforcer" kills. This is the Love/Hate, Life/Death syndrome. Love/Hate is the double-edged sword of the Binder; it cuts both ways; one kills the other. The "Guardian" and the "Enforcer" continually stand "back to back" in denial of each other. Hence, "Back to back they faced each other, drew their (double-edged) swords and shot each other" ... (arrows of "Love" and swords of "Hate")

... "Love" kills "Hate," and "Hate" kills "Love." The "Guardian" kills the "Enforcer" and the "Enforcer" kills the "Guardian." The "Enforcer" is the slave of the "Guardian"; both are constantly at war with each other.

This is an insidious state of madness. Mormonism is not the benign institution it is advertised to be.

*   *

Numbness – Death of Feelings – Self Loathing

(This young man (and his companion) was sent home from his mission for having a Thanksgiving Dinner with Elders in a neighboring town.)

"As my plane crossed the Atlantic I felt like a condemned man. Or worse, since I was convinced that I was bound to become a Son of Perdition. ... I was destined to join that handful cast into dark and everlasting space with our unexpiated sins forever weighing on our souls. ... After I arrived in Georgia I lost, for several months to follow, my ability to enjoy the taste of food, or to appreciate music, or see a movie without assuming for myself the guilt that should have been reserved for the villain. Even a Walt Disney movie like '101 Dalmatians' tapped feeling of fear and self-loathing."   Post #23 *See: Stages 5, 6, 7, #23*

The Bound, required to have One Mind with the Binder, accepts the projections the Binder sends to him. The Bound becomes the mirror image of the Binder through projection.

*   *

Death of Feelings – "Love"

"If you can break through the 'best two years of my life,' ... you can get most returned missionaries to admit the truth: an LDS mission has more to do with salesmanship and numbers than it does with heart and soul. ... My mission president ... was consumed with increasing the 'numbers' to the point of ignoring the fragile emotional health of the children (I use that term purposely) that served as his proselytizing force. One of his favorite expressions? 'You're sucking a hind teat, Elder!'"   Post #26

*   *

Self-Loathing – Dehumanization

"The church taught that the Holy Spirit could protect you from temptation. With the Holy Spirit and faith, you could cast off the 'natural man.' 'Lead me not into temptation, but deliver me from evil' just didn't seem to be working for me. Of course, I blamed it on myself and thought there was something wrong with me. I thought I was perverted. I felt evil inside. I hated myself."   Post # 28 *See: Stages 1, 2 – 3, 4, 5, #28*

> *The only total way the "natural man" can be "cast off" is through physical castration. Mormonism, through pathological mental and emotional conditioning ... through the "Spirit," seeks to psychologically castrate both men and women; they become neutered, sexless ... neither male nor female ... a reflection of the self-contained male-female Adam who "begot" Eve. In that "pre-mortal" condition they were both ignorant of sex which, in the temple ceremony today, is reenacted by each member actor as they become another Adam or another Eve ... before the "fall," that is, when ignorant of sex, and therefore "pure." The effect of this conditioning is to try to benumb ... through "guilt" ... all sensual perceptions by fostering a hatred of the body and labeling it "evil."*

*   *

Blind, Deaf, Dumb, unable to Move

"I had never had a Christian tell me I was lost, not even while I was a missionary. Yet, I was as convinced of it as I could be and still know that God had grace. I did not see myself as spiritually dead – only blind, deaf, dumb and unable to move. How I wished to see and hear, and yet I could not!! God's silence even led me to doubt His love for me."   Post #38 *See: Stages 2 – 3, 4, 5, 6, 7, 8, #38*

> *This young man was caught in every Stage of The Pattern because of his sincerity. The "damned if you do, and damned if you don't" dilemma paralyzes the mind with its no-win snare and leaves the individual confused, full of self-blame and a stranger to his own legitimate needs.*

*   *

Psychological Cannibalism

"The more I questioned and tried to make sense of my life, I would have these awful feelings of anxiety because I was sure Satan was slowly tempting me 'into carnal security' and other such nonsense. The years of conditioning had solidified a great many anxieties in me. What angers me now is not what was conditioned into me, but what was not allowed to grow because of that conditioned and paranoid environment, namely a sense of well-being and security, a sense of true self, and self esteem. I've realized many years later now that much of my anxiety had little to do with Satan and a lot to do with defense mechanisms being shaken and pulled at. Defense mechanisms that shored up a great amount of turbulence and instability at home and in my young life, and years of cruel emotional treatment by this religion." Post #65 *See: Stages 7, 8, #65*

*   *

Psychological Cannibalism – Loss of the Personal in all Relationships and the Will to Live

"Throughout the whole of my adult life, I have run and hid, side-stepped and avoided, fabricated and lied to avoid upsetting mom and dad. This has been the predominant mode of operation in this and most Mormon families as long as I can remember. There is no open, free exchange of ideas in this family because it's taboo to upset mom and dad or question the dogmatic status-quo. You don't share your personal beliefs, fears, doubts, dreams, concepts, theories, discoveries, attitudes, opinions, and views because it will just upset mom and dad. You keep your personal, family, and marital problems locked tightly away from prying eyes until they fester into a cancer that eats away at your will to live because you don't want to upset mom and dad." Post #67 *See: Stage 8, #67*

*   *   *

"Every principle for personal growth, once institutionalized, shifts from serving as a vehicle for self-actualization to serving the actualization of the vehicle itself. We are no longer nurtured, but managed."

~Matt Berry, "A Human Strategy," #17

Part III

My Mormon Crisis

Thoughts of Suicide

"Yes, the leaders are *inspired,* "But, no, they are "*only human.*"

"Yes, have *only Faith*," "But," no, you should *already* "*know.*"

My first Mormon crisis occurred several years before my awakening to The Pattern. My depression was deepening, and I found myself plunging down into my "black hole" again. I had always tried to hide my depression from my family with a "happy face" and positive outlook. Thanks to my non-Mormon father, and his positive outlook on life, I survived and even fooled myself sometimes by remembering his words and his example. Like all Mormon women that I knew, I felt that I was just not trying hard enough; if I was unhappy, it was my own fault somehow. This latest depression began directly after my husband's confession that he had not been sexually continent prior to our marriage; I had thoughts of suicide. (At that time I did not know about his liaisons during our marriage also. His guilt and self-hatred for these betrayals ... which he could not acknowledge ... he projected to me, which was the unknown subliminal cause of my recurring depressions. Binders eventually hate those whom they have deceived and mistreated, but at the same time this hate is covered up with the pretended label – "Love." This label in Mormonism is synonymous with "Duty" – "Thou <u>shalt</u> love." This is the "Voluntary" union ... the Love/Hate of Stage 8. This kind of a relationship is inherent in the The Pattern used in Mormonism.)

I couldn't pull myself out of my depression this time. I decided to see my Stake President whom I had known for years. I needed help desperately. I arrived at the chapel at the appointed time and was invited into his office. He sat behind his desk ... with arms, elbows, clenched hands and body, leaning slightly forward. I'll never forget that moment. I sat in a chair facing him; I didn't know what to do or how to begin. He finally asked me why I had asked for the meeting. I came right out with it. I said that I was frightened because I had suicidal thoughts. He leaned closer towards me and looking directly into my eyes, asked, "Marion, what *terrible* thing have you *done?*" At that moment, there was a flash of light, an explosion in my head, literally. Here was this man of "God," who held an office as a "spiritual" leader, with "spiritual" insight, and *he had judged me without knowing the reason why* I wanted to commit suicide. I had been pre-judged "guilty" without his knowing any of the facts. He was my accuser, the jury, the judge, and had just executed ... *himself* ... *as an "inspired" leader.* (This Stake President had blindly punished me for having been punished. Stage 7.)

I had been in the church for over 40 years and had not asked for anything before this. I had not tested any of the claims in Mormonism because I hadn't questioned anything. I left his office as hurriedly as I could, angry, shocked, but at the same time, strangely lighter. The bond had been broken between this leader ... all church leaders ... and myself. The bond was lessening, too, in my marriage. However, I thought that what happened to my husband in the Navy was many years ago; we had six children now; my whole life had been and was still invested in this marriage and my family. I was sadder but wiser, but was determined to question everything from then on. That was the very beginning. I still knew nothing; I was truly ignorant. I was beginning to think, however, that I was not really stupid, as I had been led to believe. I also had been led to think the enemy was "out there" and to ignore anything that wasn't in Mormonism; in that respect, I was *ignor*-ant. Later, I would be blamed by my husband for having been "*so naive.*"

Members of the church, and women especially, are programmed with "milk" images and labels; in fact, we have all been commanded to ...("Yes,") ... become as little children, have faith, and trust in our husbands and leaders (Stage 2 – 3), ("But") ... then, later, we are accused of being "naive," as if to say "Grow up, you're not a child," or, "You should have known that we are *only human* (Stage 6). The two stages create *a double-bind*, used over and over again, by the "Shepherd" who says, *"Trust me!"* ... "Don't question authority," and the "Wolf" who says, *"Be responsible; you 'chose' to be ignorant."* Another double-bind. If you *trust* you are *naive* (deficient). If you use *reason* you have lost your *faith*.

This is an example of the Binder having it both ways. To bind another to him there must be complete faith and trust; reason is the "enemy." When he (or the Mormon church) feels threatened however, the Binder *claims* reality and reason (for himself) ... as *his* defense. And because reason, for the Bound, has not been allowed to mature the Bound is then defenseless in face of the Binder's mysterious "intelligence."

*   *   *

Duty and Meaning: Where our duty has no personal meaning we wish for a little understanding from our superiors. But they can spare none, for without our duty, their meaninglessness is exposed.

~ Matt Berry, "A Human Strategy," #18

My Awakening to The Pattern

My conscious awakening to this pattern began 30 years after my 1950 marriage. It happened during my divorce. As has been seen in previous posts, an awakening usually begins with a crisis of some kind, created by questioning values which were previously taken for granted. The act of questioning usually begins when the danger of questioning is no longer a threat, when one has time or is forced by a crisis *to think*. In my case, I left my husband and the church, each because of a crisis; I was dying emotionally and intellectually. I didn't know the exact cause of my deep depression; it was *felt,* rather than known, as a dark cloud over my mind, which was causing a general emotional/intellectual numbness which would send me spiraling down into a deep depression, into what I called my "Black Hole." At one such time, I had thoughts of suicide.

My dilemma was, that I knew I would continue to "die" if I stayed with my husband and within the church; they had become one as far as my depression was concerned. But, at the same time, I felt I would "die" if I left – a double-bind. I decided that I could do more for my 6 children, and myself, if I left, than I could if I stayed in my living-death situation; I would be doing *more* harm by staying. At least, I thought, I had a chance to survive if I left.

The Painting

This awakening experience contained many stages of The Pattern. However, at that time, I had no knowledge of the double-bind or any kind of a pattern. Hence, there were no stages for me to recognize. I am, in retrospect, showing the stages now, as they occurred in this one awakening experience.

Stage 1. The Problem – Anxiety

I had filed for a divorce. It was a painful process for both my husband and myself, causing great anxiety.

Stage 2. Agreement – Solution

In California law there is an equal division of property and assets. Each party has a lawyer, and each party is required to supply information needed to the lawyers. There was an agreement to supply the information each of us had.

Stage 3. "Yes, but ..." – Ambiguity – Identity Crisis

We had a valuable painting that was being stored. Since it had not been purchased for personal use, we needed to sell it in order to divide the assets. Arrangements needed to be made. It had been some time since the purchase of the painting, and essential details needed to be reviewed. My husband had been involved in the paper work and the details concerning it; he had these *means* at his office. I called him on the telephone to get feedback on how we should proceed. "Yes" (he knew it had to be done), "But"... he was "just *too* busy to *deal* with it."

Stage 4. Double-Bind – Reversal

I had no experience in the marketing of valuable antiques, which applied to this painting, but I offered to try to sell it just the same. I questioned him in regard to the essential information he had that I needed in order to get started. I asked, "Where is it?"

"What is its value?" ... basic questions. Suddenly, he became very angry and exploded with, "How should I know? I don't care about *things*!"

I was stunned. It was as if a knife had pierced my heart, and simultaneously, there was an explosion inside my brain ... literally. These are not poetic statements; both were physical effects from the double-bind shock I had just received. I felt as if a short-circuit of some kind had occurred, and/or that a fully charged mental connection of some kind had been made; this erupted into a question, "What *do* you care about, ... *people?*" I felt I had been violated ... mentally and emotionally *raped* ... and *at the same time*, I felt an unearned sense of "guilt," for some unknown "crime."

Gradually, as I tried to figure out what was wrong with the "reasoning" in that experience, I discovered that no matter what I would choose, I would be "guilty." I didn't know at that time that there was any such thing a double-bind. But I recognized the *feelings* that were attached to this experience ... feelings that I had felt before but from which I could find no escape ... feelings that belonged in my "Black Hole" of depression. This time it was different; this was the beginning of making connections between my perceptions and my thinking brain.

The Double-Bind – Reversal of Roles

If I *didn't* take the full responsibility of selling the painting, I would be "guilty" of keeping him away from his clients, and I would be "selfish." (*"Others" needed him more than I did.*)

If I *did* take full responsibility, I would be "guilty" of being "mercenary," because I "cared for *things*." *(Again, I would be labeled "selfish.")*

I was damned if I *didn't* sell the painting, and I was damned if I *did.*

This, as I later found out, was a way of "justifying" a situation by attacking a person's character instead of facing the facts ... the *agreement.* This double-bind denied the main issue by reversing *his* guilt of reneging on an agreement into *my* being *"selfish."* He was washed *"white,"* and I was painted *"black."*

Stage 5. Denial – Dehumanization – Humiliation

In addition, the reversal in Stage 4 erased all previous history and facts. He had all the necessary information I would need if I were to take over his portion of the responsibility, and he effectively refused me the *means* of accomplishing what he was forcing me to do. Whichever choice I would make, I would be "guilty" ... plus, he was denying me the means of doing it (*doubly* punishing me).

The question, "How should I know?" was an explicit denial that he knew anything about the painting; he was saying, "What painting?"

I was also dehumanized, in that he insinuated that I cared for *"things"* and myself, more than I cared for other people. He had put me in the category with *"things"; I was "inhuman" and "non-caring"* (the projection of his treatment of me).

If he really had cared for *people*, he would have cared enough *to act* on that implied claim; he would have done his share in selling the painting. As the "Shepherd," he *claims* the label "human"; ... as the "Wolf," in real life, he destroys the human aspect of others, then projects and accuses the Bound of not being *"human."* Again, the "Shepherd" and the "Wolf" stand back to back, neither of them "recognizing" the other. What the "Shepherd" *says* is the opposite of what the "Wolf" *does.*

Stage 6. "Not I, but, you ..." are "guilty." – Demonization

The above event also included an accusation through his "Wolf" projection. He was saying, "This is *your* problem, *not mine,"* or "It was your idea to sell the painting, not mine." "You *chose* to sell it." This is an extension of Stage 3, the **"Yes, but."** The **"Yes"** of the "Shepherd" having been dropped, I was forced to accept the **"But,"** and then was accused by the "Wolf" of having originally *"chosen,"* for *"selfish"* reasons, to sell the painting. This was a reversal of my identity, from being an <u>equal partner</u> in the sale of the painting to being a demonized *"bitch"* ... a projection of his *"Wolf"* personality ... *because I had asked questions* for a solely *"selfish"* reason.

Stage 7. Abandonment – Punished for Being Punished

I had been completely abandoned, and the joint agreement (Stage 2) was "as if it had never been." He was doubly punishing me for *choosing* to leave him, for not accepting *more* of his punishment ... for not being "obedient" to his double-binds, as I had been in the past. I was becoming *"uncontrollable."*

*   *   *

This is the same treatment members of the church receive when they wake up to see the mental and emotional violence hidden within its doctrine and decide to question or to leave it. They are punished for *seeing* that they are being punished unjustly.

This Pattern in Mormonism began with Joseph Smith's *personal* mind-set, which he used in his own marriage. He then put this Pattern into writing as "scripture" ... as "commandments." It became church "doctrine." Today this church "doctrine" trickles down into the personal marriage relationships of members of his Patriarchal church.

Mormonism is kept in a circular Closed System in prescribing Joseph Smith's *"Holy* (double-bind) *scriptures"* as a cure for *all* ills and "sin" – in place of ***reasonable questioning of real life problems,*** **problems that can't be solved or cured until they are dis-*covered*.** That is why Mormonism fears the rational mind and uses this Pattern of Denial. **You can't fight what you can't *see*.** For the Pattern to work, **human perceptions** must be psychologically destroyed, gradually ... by fear and guilt, so that the brain can be short-circuited and prevented from functioning ... from reasoning.

True Believing Mormons are *programmed* to act as Binder or Bound in a Pattern that repeats continuously, so that, *essentially,* nothing is ever new, causing apathy, if not atrophy, of the brain. As with actors and actresses on a stage, the script and the actions have all been prescribed and memorized but without the underlying meanings of the plot really understood. We are told that the *meanings* in the "doctrine," the "meat" (the *"unofficial"* that is *ever changing*), are *mysteries we cannot know in this life* because as "little children" we are not *ready* for them; we must live only on the *"official* milk," the "official" doctrine (that *never* changes) of *obedience* and *sacrifice of Self* ... and must follow unquestioningly our *official* leaders.

The tragedy of my marriage was that neither one of us was *really there.* Reality had been hidden so deeply as to be only felt as an unknown longing, which could not be seen nor identified, and therefore never satisfied. This is *the basis* of the low to high grade depressions from which Mormons suffer ... *the loss of personal Identity.*

It is a tragedy that Mormonism uses The Pattern, consciously or unconsciously, in destroying the possibilities and the actual killing of the very values they ostensibly profess to love and advertise, ... *love* and *understanding* in marriage and family relationships. I cannot blame my husband or myself for the failure of our marriage. We were both caught in the drama of The Pattern, as Binder and Bound, playing for real, unreal roles assigned to us in Mormonism. It is not unlike an actor playing the part of Othello night after night, then, eventually, believing that he *is* Othello, strangling in reality the actress-wife he "loves."

*   *   *

*"The object is not to forgive in spite of oneself. The object is a higher degree of **clarity**. That this state "forgives" is coincidental and accounts for the misunderstanding. To forgive or not to forgive was never the conflict. The true conflict was one of level: whether one had the strength to climb above the lower conflict, to exist from a higher point of view."*

~ *Matt Berry, "A Human Strategy," #172*

Part IV

Summary – How to Free Oneself from The Pattern

The Words of the Shepherd VS the Action of the Wolf

If a person is living in an invisible prison yet believes he or she is free, no effort will be made to escape. The prison of the Double-Bind has the facade of the Real World in every way, inasmuch as it *claims* the beauties of the Real World but insidiously *destroys* that which it professes to love; only the "Shepherd" who *speaks beautiful Words* is seen; the *"Wolf,"* who in *Action* destroys, remains hidden. The Bound person wants to believe the beautiful claims and therefore trusts the "Shepherd" blindly. To see the "Wolf" is to awake to the mask of the "Shepherd" and to realize that they are really two aspects of *one person,* the Binder *with a dual mind* who can only establish a *love/hate relationship*, a relationship in which the Binder and the Bound both lose.

The Results of the Shepherd/Wolf Syndrome

This drama is an unending one until it is seen; it is circular and repeats in many guises. Experienced over a prolonged length of time the mind becomes indifferent to it inasmuch as there is, on the surface, no way to grasp it; there are no logical connections for the brain to find; they have been short-circuited. Apathy eventually sets in because the results always end in love/hate judgments of unearned guilt which must be punished by the Binder for the Bound's "own good." The Bound is always left with some underlying unfathomable depression and becomes trapped in mental chaos and undefined emotional pain ... which is then denied because the truth is too unbelievable. The greater the fraud, the greater is the denial of it and therefore the greater becomes the bond to the Binder. There is no greater fraud than to have had your real world turned upside-down ... your humanity and identity stolen, in short, *your life* ... under the guise of *right-eousness.*

The Shepherd's "Beautiful" (*fraudulent*) Words

The Binder, in order to keep the Bound enslaved and capable of continued servitude, *gives praise* for blind obedience; *praise* becomes the Bound's *one* consolation and expectation ... which however, is tenuous; it is followed by the futility that try as the Bound might, it is never possible to reach both the state of perfection of the *adult* <u>and</u> childhood *"innocence"* ... *at the same time;* in either case, something is always "not quite right." "Yes," you obeyed *(praised as an adult)* ..."But," the results weren't 'good' enough" (*"guilt" for not taking responsibility as an adult,* hence, still the *child you were <u>commanded</u> to be*). This is another example of the *Double-Bind, a* circular Pattern that prolongs the short circuiting of the brain. It is *un-thinkable.*

The More the Binder Takes, the Less the Binder has of His Own

The Binder lives with a compulsion, a hunger that can never be filled; this emptiness is projected to the Bound which she/he nevertheless is expected impossibly to fill. Lacking an integral, singular, self-identity the Binder lives through others by the theft of *their* identities. This is what I call psychological cannibalism. A Binder can only take, he cannot give of himself in that he has no self of his own to give. That being said, however, we cannot totally blame the Binder, because he himself had previously been robbed of his own identity by another Binder leader. He *does suffer* greatly, but He denies the source of His suffering; this He projects to the Bound who is then punished for "punishing" Him!

A Closed System, the Omission of Love

It is never meant that the Bound should win, only to lose; the Binder *thinks* he always wins and never loses. He sits in the driver's seat of a cart; the Bound pulls the cart in order to reach the "carrot (*of love*) on the end of the stick" which the Binder holds just beyond reach of the Bound. The tragedy is that the Binder is further away from the "carrot" of love than the Bound is. He keeps from others the very values he longs for himself; intimacy and love are kept at a distance and through the Pattern those possibilities are eventually destroyed for both; they become the unattainable in this life (hence, the promise of love in the *next* life). It is this underlying longing for *reality and love* being held at a distance and never attained that binds the Bound and the Binder together. Reality, love and trust belong in the Real World; the Binder and the Bound live in the fabricated, closed, circular world of *"waiting" for their turn to get the "golden ring" on the Merry-Go Round of The Pattern.*

The Difficulty of the Binder to Awaken

It is usually the Bound who wakes up first, if at all; the Binder is less likely to make any effort whatsoever because he believes he has everything to gain by remaining a Binder and nothing to lose; he is also supported by many other Binders ... (this is especially the case with the Brotherhood in the tribal hierarchy of the Mormon Priesthood).   Underpinning this support is a unified stratagem of denial which is maintained through silence, a result of taking "sacred oaths" which are not to be revealed under the extreme punishment of death.   I am speaking here mostly of leaders, not all male members of the church who hold the Priesthood in Mormonism are true Binders. Most are the Bound who also take oaths but are humbled to the point where "they should not seek to obtain a leadership position," for that would be *coveting.* They are to obey other Binders ... to look up to the Shepherd Leaders who will guide them ... under the principles of

The Pattern, which always remains a mystery to them. The esoteric meanings are reserved for the top "elite" leaders. Those lower in the hierarchy could rightly be called "pawns"... playing the "game" but outside the stratagem ... "Don't think ... just do what I say and fight *our* 'enemies.'" They are the "Rank and File."

Two Ways to Break the Chain of Deception

Members of the church are told by their Binder-Leaders that they live in the only "True" world ... that the world "outside" of Mormonism is the "evil enemy"; as a result they live in fear of the Real World and readily *volunteer* to become "pawns." There are two ways to break the chain which creates this reversed view of the world. One is through education and the desire to know (*which is counteracting the Shepherd*); the other is through a personal crisis that forces some kind of action (*against the Wolf*). The first is in *arresting* the Identity Crisis trap ... the Shepherd's "**Yes** ... *but* ... *I* ... *can't*" of Stage 3 ... through *conscious choice*; the second is in *rejecting* the Wolf's Force trap ... the "Not I, *but* you"... in Stage 6. Both are pivotal Stages.

Fearless Questioning and Claiming Your Right to Know

Stages 3 and 6 both involve the *self*-motivation to question and to understand the problem. The Binder would answer to the first questioning of the "Yes, But" of Stage 3 with *"Trust me."* (That is, "Don't question. The thinking has already been done *for you*.") Likewise, the Leader states, "God's mind is not your mind." (That is, "There is no *need* to think; have *faith* alone in God's *incomprehensible* mind.") The fact is that if you *faithfully* obey the Binder without ever questioning, there will never be an escape from The Pattern because awakening from The Pattern depends on *the awakening of the mind* to openly question ... *to think* on one's own; it includes *overcoming the fear* of the Binder who is applying *force through intimidation and threat* for you to obey only Him ... which demands a *"no-mind"* brain.

Again, *the cause* of the problem is the chaotic Pattern which reverses reality by short-circuiting the mind; *the cure* then used to remove the pain is more of the same through striving to achieve the state of *total* "no-mind"; the *cause* becomes the *"cure!"* It is the *Wolf and the Shepherd* as the *Cause and the Cure* which keeps The Pattern going. Once this is seen, you don't *buy* either of them. You leave ... to let the Binder wake up (hopefully) to start feeding himself.

The Weakness of the Binder-Wolf

The Binder's power is threatened when you *claim your own identity* ... your own mind, perceptions, and feelings; *the Binder's power depends on the theft of your identity!* He cannot create on his own! He becomes weak and powerless without the identities upon which He feeds; his greatest fear is to be abandoned and for his Bound captives to escape. His modus operandi, under the means of projection, is to punish others with that which he fears the most ... *abandonment.* Ironically, in the end ... if he is "successful" ... all of his projections boomerang back to him in that he has killed that upon which he fed.

Deceptions Used by the Binder-Shepherd

The Binder must keep his stratagem *hidden by denial*, and the only way to accomplish that is to *prohibit your ability to question* ... through *fear which he deems* is *"love,"* for he does this, he says, *"for your own good."* The Binder demands *blind obedience*; disobedience brings *punishment.* The Bound is *"saved"* from punishment *through fear* of punishment by being *obediently submissive.* In being *saved* by the Binder-Savior, the Bound is *expected to be "grateful" for* His *"mercy"* which leads to a *"voluntary" union with the Binder's mind.*

The antidote to fear is *to be fearless in questioning in order to cut the bond* between Binder and Bound <u>through reason</u>. Once The Pattern is truly seen, it is possible to cut this knot *surgically.* Before it is truly seen, leaving is usually the result of untying it fact by fact, gradually. Personally, I began with the latter; I had to *grow my own brain* to where I could regain my *natural* ability to use it as it was designed to function. The nature of the brain is to make connections that can identify and verify our own perceptions. If we are denied the choice *to see, hear,* or *identify,* the brain is short-circuited before questioning can begin, and thus connections are left to whatever fills the void ... in this case, the *preconceived* Pattern.

Cutting or untying The Pattern is the true process of being <u>re</u>-*born,* of <u>dis</u>-covering what had been stolen. You begin *growing* your own brain ... making new neural connections, *literally.*

I would like to point out again that this Pattern is not only found in Mormonism; it can also be found in many disciplines and other fundamentalist type churches in varying degrees. This is very important to realize because if you finally "escape" from Mormonism, the tendency is to think that the problem only resides there. To free yourself from The Pattern in Mormonism can also free you from becoming entangled in it outside of Mormonism as well, but only if you are aware of its stages.

The first requirement is gaining the knowledge and understanding of the way The Pattern works, plus *vigilance* in detecting it wherever it is found.

Freeing oneself from The Pattern is like preparing soil for the planting of new seeds that produce nutritious foods for the body, emotions and brain, and for colorful flowers that create more beauty in our lives. First, the weeds of The Pattern must be *seen* and pulled out, then the soil of the mind must be cultivated *through reason* and the seeds of new understandings planted in anticipation of healthy increase ... The Law of *Increasing* Returns. It is a process that produces *quality* and *true Joy* ... because it is *earned.* True *peace* comes from *owning one's own mind* ... having *Self*-control and Self-*respect* ... in short, in discovering our own unique *Identity.* When this point is realized you "absolve yourself to yourself." *(Ralph Waldo Emerson)*

This is accomplished through vigilance and through the positive *repetition* of this process. In *conscious* (chosen) repetition, based on the understanding of the process, the reward is greater and greater freedom, and the means to true Love of Self and Others; it is the very opposite of the negative, rote, repetitive Pattern of The Double-Bind which *destroys* Identity ... our Integrity. One could define the positive growth process of *repetition* as *human behavior* ... understood ... and applied with *constancy of purpose* ... the real roots of the meaning of life and happiness. It is not passively abstract; it is active and substantial. It is the *human Self* ... *in the real world.* "*Self*"-*behavior, Self-reliance,* is *confirmation* of unique *Identity.*

*   *   *

"There are no magic words, just as there are no instant values. The confusion arises when we think we are scientists etching a complex formula on a chalkboard, when in reality we should be simple farmers weeding and cultivating a garden of preferred habits and stimuli."

~Matt Berry, "A Human Strategy," #279

"For every lie I kill, I find another innocent truth grazing in the meadow."

~ Ibid, #283

Recommended Reading – Web Sites

Recommended Reading – Web Sites

Additional essays on *The Pattern of The Double-Bind in Mormonism* can be found on the author's Web Site http://www.threegraces.com/AboveThe DoubleBind/ which include the following:

The Pattern in Marriage and Family Relationships
Parallels – My Marriage – Emma's and Joseph's (Smith)
The Core of the Problem
The Mosaic Law – Commandments 1 – 10
The Passion For Life After Mormonism
The Art of Integrity
Art – The Companion Of Integrity
Vigilance Through Strength

For those who are interested in the origins of The Pattern, and where it can be found other than in Mormonism, there is another planned series of essays now in progress. Notification will be posted on the above Web Site under "What's New."

While my essays are about The Nature of The Pattern of The Double-Bind, Matt Berry has written about his journey in *"A Human Strategy,"* a strategy which he used in rising above The Double-Bind and Mormonism. A review of this book can be seen at Web Site http://www.human.addr.com/

Matt has also written a penetrating new book – *"Self-behaviorism: The Role of Repetition in the Meaning of Life"* – on living a reclaimed life in the *Real* World. It was through a positive behavioral repetition that I was successful in leaving The Pattern ... thanks to Matt's earnest investigations in this area that he shared with me. His book contains this *positive* use of repetition ... the direct opposite of the negative repetition contained in The Pattern. It may be viewed at http://www.upublish.com/books/berry2.htm

Eric Kettunen's Web Site *Recovery From Mormonism* (from which the Posts in this book were taken and which made this book possible) has been changed to *Freedom From Mormonism* and may be seen at: http://www.exmormon.org/ There are many more stories posted on Eric's site since I did my research for this book.

For additional information on almost everything on Mormonism and for exploring avenues of Reason there are these sites by "rpcman." *(Post #12)*

- *Honest Intellectual Inquiry*:
  http://www.california.com/~rpcman/MO.HTM
- *2 Think*: http://www.2think.org/
- *Mormonism and the LDS Church:* http://www.lds-mormon.com/

Recommended highly is Ralph Waldo Emerson's essay on *Self-Reliance.* http://www.california.com/~rpcman/emerson.htm

NOTES

Printed in the United States
98210LV00005B/106/A

9 781581 127393